Dave G Biogra

The Man Behind the Drum Kit

By Arthur Culin Hilbmann

TABLE OF CONTENTS

PART 5
LIVING

CHAPTER 1
Joan Jett's Bedtime Stories

CHAPTER 2
The Daddy-Daughter Dance

CHAPTER 3
The Wisdom of Violet

INTRODUCTION

Increase the volume

I sometimes forget how old I am. My intellect and heart appear to perform this terrible joke on me, tricking me with the false sense of youth by welcoming the world every day through the idealistic, mischievous eyes of a rebellious child who finds delight and admiration in the simplest, most fundamental things. Though a single glance in the mirror reminds me that I am no longer the small boy with a cheap guitar and a stack of albums, practicing alone for hours on end in the hopes of one day breaking free from the limits and expectations of my suburban Virginia, Wonder Bread existence. No. I was requested to sing at the 12-12-12 Hurricane Sandy relief concert in New York City many years ago. It included the Mount Rushmore of rock and roll lineups, including McCartney, the Rolling Stones, the Who, Roger Waters, and countless other household names. A promoter approached me at one point and asked if I would join some of the most legendary artists in the greenroom to take photos with certain fans who had donated huge sums of money to the cause.

I gladly consented, making my way through the maze of backstage passageways, visualizing a room full of rock and roll history, all standing in an elementary school photo formation, nothing but leather jackets and British accents. As I walked in, I was astonished to see only two of the performers, who were standing at opposite ends of the room. One had the gleaming appearance of a brand-new luxury automobile. It may seem corny, but I glimpsed my future in a flash. I made the decision right then and there to become the latter. That I would celebrate the coming years by accepting the toll they would exact on me. That I would aspire to be the rusted-out hot rod, regardless of how many jump-starts I would need along the road. After all, not everything needs a shine. If you leave a Pelham Blue Gibson Trini Lopez guitar in its case for fifty years, it will still look brand new. But if you hold it in your hands, expose it to the light, let it breathe, sweat on it, and fucking PLAY it, the finish will eventually develop a distinct colour. And each instrument ages in its own unique way. That, to me, is beauty. The road-worn beauty of personality, time, and wisdom, not the sparkle of prefabricated perfection.

My memory has somehow remained substantially intact. I've always judged my life in musical increments rather than months or years since I was a child. To remember a specific moment and place, my mind faithfully relies on songs, albums, and bands. I could tell you who, what, where, and when from the first few notes of each song that has creeped from a speaker to my soul, from seventies AM radio to every microphone I've stood before. Alternatively, from my soul to your speakers. Some people's memories are awakened by taste, whereas others are activated by sight or scent. Mine is activated by sound and plays like an incomplete mixtape ready to be transmitted. Though I am not a collector of "stuff," I do collect moments. As a result, my life flashes before my eyes and via my ears every day. As best I can, I've captured some of them in this book. Of course, these recollections from my life are filled with music. They can also be quite loud at times. AMP IT UP. JOIN ME IN LISTENING.

PART 1
Establishing the Scene

CHAPTER 1
DNA Doesn't Lie

Harper, my eight-year-old daughter, stood there hesitantly holding a pair of my shattered drumsticks in her tiny little hands, peering at me with her large brown eyes like Cindy Lou Who from How the Grinch Stole Christmas. My middle child, my mini-me, my daughter who looks the most like me. I had expected her to be interested in music at some point, but drums? Talk about an entry-level mailroom job at the bottom of the trough! I realized as soon as we walked into my office that I had never taken official drum lessons and hence had no idea how to teach someone to play the drums. The closest I'd gotten to systematic music tuition was a few hours with an incredible jazz drummer named Lenny Robinson, whom I used to see perform every Sunday afternoon at a local Washington, DC jazz club called One Step Down.

Unlike the conventions of modern music (which I despised at the time, like the boy from The Omen at church), I found beauty and vitality in the chaotic tapestry of jazz composition. Sometimes it's structured, sometimes it's not. But, above all, I admired Lenny Robinson's drumming. This was something I'd never seen at a punk rock event before. He made it all look so easy (I now know it's not) with his thunderous attitude and graceful perfection. For me, it was a musical awakening. I'd learned to play the drums by ear on unclean pillows in my bedroom and had never had somebody standing over me telling me what was "right" or "wrong," so my drumming was wild, with irregularity and feral behaviors. I WAS THE MUPPETS' ANIMAL WITHOUT THE CHOPS. Lenny was definitely trained, and I was impressed by his feel and control. Drummers such as Ivor Hanson, Earl Hudson, Jeff Nelson, Bill Stevenson, Reed Mullin, D. H. Peligro, John Wright, etc. To this day, you can hear echoes of their work in my music, with songs like "Song for the Dead" by

Queens of the Stone Age, "Monkey Wrench" by Foo Fighters, and even Nirvana's "Smells Like Teen Spirit" (to name a few). All of those musicians appeared to be worlds apart from Lenny's scene, but they all shared the same sensation of beautiful, controlled chaos that I enjoyed every Sunday at One Step Down. That's what I worked hard for.

We were truly friends in the age of Generation X, divorce, and dysfunction. They still are! My mother went to me after a few baskets of fries and a few sets from Lawrence Wheatley's quartet and asked, "David, would you go up and sit in with the band as a birthday present to me?" I don't remember precisely what my first reaction was, but it was probably something along the lines of "ARE YOU OUT OF YOUR FUCKING MIND?" I reluctantly consented and carefully rose from our small table, threading my way through the crowded gathering of jazz fans to the coffee-stained sign-up page near the stage. It was divided into two columns: "Name" and "Instrument." I skimmed over the names of other seemingly competent musicians on the list and hastily scribbled "David Grohl— drums." I felt as if I had signed my own death warrant. In a haze, I staggered back to our table, feeling all eyes on me as I sat down and immediately began sweating through my ripped jeans and punk rock T-shirt. Soon after, Lawrence Wheatley's rich baritone drawl blared over the PA speakers, announcing the terrifying words that still haunt me to this day: "Ladies and gentlemen, please welcome... on the drums... David Grohl."

I nervously stood to a scattering of applause, which rapidly faded as the audience realized I wasn't a seasoned jazz star, but rather a skinny suburban punk with strange hair, muddy Converse Chucks, and a T-shirt that screamed KILLING JOKE. The dread on the band's faces as I approached the stage gave the impression that the Grim Reaper himself was on his way. When I walked onto the platform, the great Lenny Robinson handed me his sticks and I hesitantly sat on his throne, and for the first time, I saw the room through his eyes. These poor musicians had unintentionally allowed me to give my mother a birthday gift she would never forget (much to the chagrin of about seventy-five paying customers), which meant more to me than any standing ovation I could have dreamed for.

Humbled, I walked back to our hors d'oeuvres table in shame, believing that I had a long, long way to go before I could call myself a true drummer. That fateful afternoon sparked a spark in me. Inspired by my failure, I decided that I needed to learn how to play the drums from someone who knew what they were doing, rather than attempting to figure it out on my bedroom floor all by myself. And there was only one person who could show me how: the great Lenny Robinson. Our thirteen-hundred-square-foot Springfield home was far too small for a full drum set (hence the impromptu pillow practice set in my tiny bedroom), but for this special occasion I brought in the bottom-of-the-line five-piece Tama kit from my band Dain Bramage's practice space, which was nowhere near Lenny's caliber of gear. As I excitedly awaited his arrival, I uncomfortably positioned the filthy drums in front of the living room stereo and shined them up with some Windex I found under the kitchen sink, thinking that soon all the neighbors would hear him ripping it to tears... and think it was me! I couldn't believe it was occurring on the same carpet where I had spent my entire life dreaming of becoming a world-class drummer someday. It was finally happening. This was my fate. I was on my way to becoming the next Lenny Robinson, as his riffs became mine.

I had no idea it was the polar opposite of proper jazz drumming. I'm a moron. He then demonstrated a conventional hold, taking the stick in my left hand and passing it through my thumb and middle finger, as all true drumming greats had done before him, and certainly before me. This one change utterly destroyed everything I had believed I knew about drumming up until that moment, leaving me crippled behind the kit, as if I were learning to walk after a decade-long coma. He started showing me simple, single-stroke rolls on a practice pad as I strained to keep hold of the stick in this impossible new way. Right-left-right-left. Over and over, slowly hitting the pad to find a constant balance. Right-left-right-left. Again. Right-left-right-left. The class was over before I knew it, and I realized that at thirty dollars an hour, it was probably cheaper for me to go to Johns Hopkins and become a fucking brain surgeon than to learn how to play drums like Lenny Robinson. I gave him the money and thanked him for his time, and that was the end of it. My one and only drum lesson.

As Harper played, I leaped and cheered, my heart swelled with joy, headbanging and singing along with the songs. Then I noticed something odd: her posture. Her broad back arched forward somewhat, sharp arms and narrow elbows angled forward slightly, chin elevated over the snare... and I saw it. SHE WAS A COPY OF ME PLAYING THE DRUMS WHEN SHE WAS HER AGE. I felt like I was time-traveling and having an out-of-body experience at the same time. Not only that, but my grinning doppelganger was learning to play the drums the same way I had thirty-five years before: by listening to music with her mom. But I wasn't entirely surprised. As I already stated, I was always expecting this. As I stated in the foreword to my mother's book, From Cradle to Stage, I believe that these musical impulses are present, lurking somewhere deep within the DNA strand and simply waiting to be awakened. I knew all I needed was that DNA and a lot of patience (which my mother definitely had in abundance) the day I picked up a guitar and performed Deep Purple's 'Smoke on the Water' by ear. Someone gave birth to these ears, heart, and mind. Someone who shared my passion for music and song. I was given a genetic symphony that was just ready to be performed. It only took that spark." Harper's "spark" had arrived the day before as she sat in her seat at the Roxy nightclub on Sunset Boulevard, watching her older sister, Violet, perform her debut concert at the tender age of eleven. Yes, I was aware of it as well.

Violet's love of music soon trained her ear to recognize pitch, key, and tone. I could hear her focusing on the tiny movements of each of her favorite singers' voices as she sang from the back seat. The Beatles' harmonies, Freddie Mercury's vibrato, Amy Winehouse's soul (probably the most memorable, as there's nothing like hearing your five-year-old kid sing "Rehab" word for word while wearing Yo Gabba Gabba! pajamas). It was obvious that she possessed the ability. It was just a matter of time before she stumbled across the spark. I sat in the audience with my family for Violet's concert at the Roxy on Sunset Boulevard, her first "official" show with her band. "Don't Stop Believin'" by Journey, "Hit Me with Your Best Shot" by Pat Benatar, and "Sweet Child O' Mine" by Guns N' Roses were my particular favorites, but I had to pause during the performance to take

12

it all in. Harper's eyes were brimming with hopes of one day being a musician, and my mother was happily witnessing another generation of her family baring their soul to a room full of strangers. The next day, my mother texted me, "Now YOU know what it's like to nervously sit in an audience as YOUR child steps onstage for the first time to follow their life passion with a funny haircut, dressed in jeans and t-shirt." She was correct. THIS WAS NOT DIVINE INSTRUCTION. THIS WAS BLOOD AND FLESH. Since then, I've played in front of thousands of people all around the world with both of my children, and each time I'm filled with a sensation similar to my mother's pride on that muggy July afternoon at One Step Down so many years ago. It is the greatest gift of my life to witness my own children's passion and courage as they take that jump, and I hope that someday their children will feel the same thrill.

CHAPTER 2
Sandi's Bereavement

Sandi was her name. She was also my first heartbreak. It was 1982, and as a gangly thirteen-year-old entering seventh grade, I was overcome with apprehensive excitement as I met all the new, strange faces at Holmes Intermediate School. Life had been confined to my lovely little North Springfield neighborhood, where I had grown up with the same kids I had known since kindergarten in our suburban maze of rolling hills and congested cul-de-sacs. North Springfield was a close-knit community of largely young families, with no genuine outsiders. Everyone knew your name, which street you lived on, and which church you attended following your messy divorce. Moving on to another school with students from diverse, remote neighborhoods seemed almost international to me. My entire childhood, I had walked the single block to my elementary school across the corner. But I had carefully planned for this following move.

It would be years before I discovered the bravery to accept my uniqueness, but at the time I was almost closed off, suppressing my interest in alternative culture for fear of being shunned by the cool kids. I went along with it, but I knew I wasn't made out for the Key Club or the football team. I was a bit of an outcast, hoping to be understood and for someone to accept the true me. Then I noticed her. Sandi was the most stunning woman I'd ever seen. Ice-blue eyes, feathery blond hair, and a smile so bright it could have charged every Tesla from Brentwood to Beijing in 1982, if Teslas had existed. She had nothing on Farrah Fawcett. Eat your heart out, Cheryl Tiegs. Derek, Bo? What about Christie Brinkley? It's not even close.

Nonetheless, I had met my match, and I couldn't stop myself from making Sandi mine. Every day, I'd rush home from school, shut my bedroom door, and write her poems and songs on my Sears Silvertone guitar, spewing my heart out to her in god-awful tunes for just her ears. She had become my inspiration, my beacon, and every waking moment was spent fantasizing about our perfect, unavoidable union. I was hopelessly in love, and my frail little heart couldn't go another day without even a smidgeon of her reciprocation. I had the feeling I was a monarch. A deity of nerds. DAVID ERIC GROHL AND I WERE NOW FORMALLY ENGAGED IN A MUTUAL RELATIONSHIP WITH THE MOST BEAUTIFUL GIRL IN THE WORLD... OR AT LEAST IN OUR GRADE. I had finally met my suburban soul mate, the love of my life, the person I would spend my golden years with, surrounded by litters of adoring grandkids. I had discovered my other half. And she had discovered hers. "You know... I'm new here... and I really don't want to get tied down." I was completely taken aback by such heinous sacrilege and paused in my tracks. Time had stopped. My thoughts became blank. I couldn't breathe because my throat was tight. My entire universe was instantly ripped from beneath my feet, and with those words slicing through my heart like a poison scythe, I was struck down and reduced to a puddle of anguish. Of course, I agreed and shrugged it off with a smile, but I was definitely dead inside. Annihilated.

I had a dream that night. I was on a massive platform, surrounded by colored lights, while I delivered a triumphant guitar solo to a sold-out crowd of adoring people, burning the fretboard with a skill never before displayed by a mortal man. I awoke with a start, and the dismal sensation of grief and dejection vanished, replaced by an inspired sense of empowerment. AS I LAY THERE STARING AT THE CEILING, IT CAME TO ME THAT MY GUITAR WAS, AFTER ALL, THE LOVE OF MY LIFE. Perhaps I didn't require

Sandi. Perhaps my Silvertone might help me repair my broken heart. Maybe I'll be able to write my way out of this mess. I was more determined than ever to realize my rock and roll ambition. The sweet sting of a love denied is powerful enough to send any scribe scurrying for pen and paper, yearning to discover beauty in the sorrow of being eighty-sixed by someone else. And, more often than not, the outcome is positive because it is genuine and fucking painful.

The sensation was obviously very different from the palpitations I'd once felt near our lockers in the fluorescent-lit hallways of intermediate school, but there was a certain joy that you can only feel when you're reunited with someone from your past, like some kind of reassurance that life really did happen. The minutes passed quickly, but it was soon time for me to get ready to go play, so I asked Sandi to remain after the gig for a bit more catch-up over a beer or two. I dashed out the door to jot down a set list and wait for the house lights to go out. I played every chord with every fiber of my being that night to thank them for a lifetime of Kodachrome memories, returning the tidal wave of love that flooded over me as we sang every song together. At one point, as I was playing a triumphant guitar solo from the stage's edge to a sea of screaming faces, blazing the fretboard to a rapturous response, I looked down and saw Sandi standing there... in the exact same spot she had been standing in the dream I had the night she broke my heart. I came to a halt when I realized I had vividly imagined this same scenario as a thirteen-year-old child thirty years previously, almost like a premonition, and now I was actually fucking living it! MY TEENAGE ROCK AND ROLL DREAM HAD COME TRUE, AS CRAZY AS IT MAY SEEM. With one exception: Sandi wasn't sobbing uncontrollably, filled with remorse for having dumped me.

CHAPTER 3
Inside, there are scars.

House after small brick house stretching for miles in a grid of groomed lawns, broken walkways, and tall white oak trees, just big enough for baby boomers to raise a family of four on their paltry federal salary. Every morning, only minutes from the nation's capital, a long line of balding men in beige overcoats and briefcases waited to be carted off to the Pentagon or other faceless, monolithic federal buildings for another day at the desk. Life here was a consistent nine-to-five routine. A Groundhog Day rat race with only a gold watch as the prize at the end. This was the comforting reward of security and stability for those misled by the "white picket fence" illusion. It was the devil's playground for a hyperactive, mischievous child like me.

I much preferred the countless outdoor adventures, such as crawling through dank drain pipes, jumping off rooftops, or throwing crab apples from the bushes beside the road (an inadvisable prank that usually resulted in a frenzied high-speed chase, with me cutting through yards and hurling chain-link fences with Olympic speed to avoid certain low-life retribution). I would cruise the streets looking for thrills from early morning till the lamps came on, until I wore holes in my special sneakers, which had been modified with a raise on the left shoe to straighten my crooked spine. However, on this particular day, I observed my two best friends, Johnny and Tae, placing golf clubs into the trunk of their father's car. Golf? I was thinking to myself. We never, ever play golf. That's some bourgeois rich-kid nonsense. We'd brought sticks! Also, rocks! And creeks teeming with crawfish! What did we need with silly headgear and plaid pants? I hurriedly dressed and skipped over to their driveway to investigate, only to discover that they had planned a family outing to the local golf course, leaving me on my own for the afternoon. Hours passed slowly until I noticed their blue Cadillac approaching up the street. I dropped what I was doing and dashed over to their house, where I found them both swinging golf clubs madly at a practice ball on a string fixed into the ground like a tiny tetherball setup.

That day, I was wearing my favorite T-shirt, a white ringer with the Superman "S" on the chest, and as I was crossing the street, I looked down at the red and yellow logo, but to my surprise, this was no longer my lovely Superman shirt. My blood, scalp, and hair had coagulated into a sticky, clumpy mess. As I made my way to my yard, I hastened my pace in panic, still feeling no pain but knowing that one drop of blood on the living room carpet may bring this scenario to a head (couldn't resist that one). I could hear my mother vacuuming inside as I climbed the few steps to the home, so instead of barging through the door in a screaming, gory mass, I stood on the stoop and gently tapped, doing anything I could to calm the impending frenzy. My poor mother's expression as she rounded the corner to find her youngest kid standing on the threshold covered in his own blood will live on in my memory. Though I was not in pain, I could feel hers. But, to be honest, this wasn't the first time. I've never shaved my head fully, but I think that behind my mop of dark brown hair is something resembling a map of the London Underground, with innumerable lines connecting in a complex network of scars. Hands, knees, fingers, legs, lips, forehead... you name it, if it's still attached to my body, it's been patched up like a rag doll. Don't be deceived by how horrific that sounds. I was always optimistic and perceived an injury as a day off from school. And I'd give anything for one of those.

I always attempted to put on my best game face so as not to bother my mother any more than life had already, and I always tried to reassure her that whatever gaping wound I had sustained was merely a scratch, no matter how many stitches were required. Call it a protection mechanism, a neurological shutoff, whatever you want, but I can only think it came from the sacrifices my mother made to raise two happy children, no matter how much suffering she faced. THE SHOW MUST, AFTER ALL, GO ON. Fortunately, my mother was not present on the night of June 12, 2015, at Gothenburg, Sweden's Ullevi stadium. It was a lovely summer evening in Scandinavia. Clear sky, a warm wind, and 50,000 Foo Fighters fans eagerly anticipating our tried-and-true two-and-a-half-hour, twenty-five-song set list. Our little band had graduated from arena to stadium level by this point, becoming a tight, well-oiled machine that banged out song after song with little respite, and I was more than comfortable entertaining an audience of this size, living out my innermost Freddie Mercury fantasies on a nightly basis.

A local promoter came into the dressing room before the show to wish me luck and remind me that I had a lot to live up to, as the one and only Bruce Springsteen had played this stadium before and the audience was so enthralled that they "split the foundation" of the massive venue. There's no need to stress! I never saw myself getting to the level of "the Boss," but I must admit, this pep talk did turn up the heat a notch. The sun was still shining brightly in the sky as we took the stage that night, and the crowd erupted as we opened with the opening chords of "Everlong" (unquestionably our most popular song). This song, which we generally save for the encore, was the perfect choice to kick off what would turn out to be our most memorable show, and we blasted through it with the fervor of a band on fire. We rapidly launched into the fast-paced rock of "Monkey Wrench" as I sprinted from one side of the stage to the other, pounding my head and soloing like a kid in his bedroom mirror with a tennis racket. Stadium stages are not only large, but also exceedingly high, so each movement is a fifty-yard dash, leaving you with little oxygen to sing the following line when you race back to the microphone. I was barely two songs into a projected two-and-a-half-hour concert, about to be dragged off the field like an injured athlete in front of 50,000 fans. These individuals had come from all around the country, spending their hard-earned money to be entertained for the evening. I was going to put on a Boss-level performance for them, darn it. "You have my promise, right now, that the Foo Fighters... we're gonna come back and finish this show..." I thought, and then blurted out the first thing that came to mind. "KEEP PLAYING!!!" I SAID TO OUR DRUMMER TAYLOR, MY BEST FRIEND AND PARTNER IN CRIME.

The opening notes of "Cold Day in the Sun," from our fifth album, echoed through the stadium to a bewildered audience as I was brought to the side of the stage. Johan Sampson, a young Swedish doctor, cut the laces of my high-top sneaker as he removed it, and my foot dropped limp to one side. I'd dislocated my ankle, shredding all of the ligaments that hold the joint together and snapping my fibula in a clean break. He glanced up at me and stated, in a heavy

Swedish accent, "Your leg is probably broken, and your ankle is dislocated, so we must put it back in right now." At that moment, all I could think of was finishing the concert for the thousands of fans who had come to see us tear this building down with our well-oiled stadium-rock machine. I saw long lines of people leaving, their hands hanging low in disappointment, cursing our name and vowing never to return. Life has a way of gifting you serendipitous, poetic moments along the way, but as my a$$ hit that chair and my guitar was placed in my lap, I burst into the bridge of "Under Pressure," singing in my best falsetto, "Chippin' around kick my brains around the floor! These are the days it never rains but it pours..." and the deafening roar of the crowd confirmed that this song and this lyric" You can't make this stuff up. It was pure delight. It was a victory. It was all about survival. Next, I launched into our song "Learn to Fly," looking down at Johan, who was kneeling in front of me, trying to support my foot as I banged my guitar back and forth, adrenaline still coursing through my veins. I noticed that he was no longer fixated in fear but was bobbing his head to the music, so I smiled and winked, "This is pretty cool, huh?"

By the time we reached the final notes of "Best of You," I realized we had reached a watershed moment in our careers. Born from the grief and sadness of our broken past, this band was a celebration of love, life, and the commitment to finding happiness in every new day. And it signified healing and survival now more than ever. I was swiftly led to a car next to the stage, and we rushed away to the hospital, accompanied by a wailing police escort. Along the way, I observed my then-six-year-old daughter, Harper, who had witnessed the entire chain of sad events, begin to cry silently.

After all, you're only as happy as your least happy child. When I arrived at the hospital, I was put in a wheelchair and sat her in my lap for the ride to the X-ray room, doing my best to make this strange experience enjoyable. Fortunately, she laughed. When I returned to my hotel in Norway that night, the pain had finally set in, and as I lay on the couch with my cast in the air, I couldn't help but remember those summer days I'd spent as a mischievous, hyperactive daredevil child, wandering the streets looking for thrills until I had holes in my sneakers, with no regard for physical consequences. Only emotional ramifications. And as I scanned the texts on my phone, I sobbed at the outpouring of love and concern from my friends in response to the news. I knew exactly what I had to do. YOU STAND UP FROM THE GROUND. YOU MAKE YOUR WAY HOME. THE SHOW MUST CONTINUE.

CHAPTER 4
Tracey Is a Punk Rocker

"Tracey, they're here!" I stood at the bottom of the long, winding staircase in the magnificent foyer of my aunt Sherry's turn-of-the-century Evanston, Illinois, mansion, eager to welcome my ultra-cool cousin Tracey with a much-anticipated hug. Tracey was family to me as much as any blood relative, even if we weren't formally related. Our 700-mile journey from Springfield, Virginia, to Evanston was no easy task. My mother, sister, and I would cram our luggage, pillows, blankets, and a cooler full of snacks into our baby-blue 1981 Ford Fiesta for the eleven-hour drive, usually stopping halfway in Youngstown, Ohio, for a few days to visit my grandparents, who lived in Warren, not far from where I was born. Driving up the Pennsylvania Turnpike into one of America's most gorgeous corners, passing over rolling hills and through long mountain tunnels, was the highlight of the year. I always looked forward to the drive, singing along to the radio with my mother from the front seat, stopping at rest stations for souvenirs, and eating sandwiches we had packed for the trip. Even as a child, I could appreciate the subtle shift in terrain as we barreled across the country into the Midwest in our tiny little car, jammed in like cosmonauts for hours on end. I can only assume that the enjoyment I had in observing the long road ahead motivated me to travel those same routes later in life.

I had a great time in Chicago. Its cosmopolitan maze of subway carriages and brick buildings appeared to be a playground of possibilities, far more thrilling than my home in Virginia's peaceful suburban surroundings. Along with Tracey, the most daring of my "cousins," there were her three older brothers, Trip, Todd, and Troy, who would always take me under their wing and show me a world outside of my own that I would never have experienced otherwise, from exploring the city to playing for hours on the warm beaches of Lake Michigan. This was Fantasy Island, Club Med, and Copacabana for me. This was also my first real feeling of independence, as I began taking the L downtown without my mother's supervision to explore the city's various corners, swiftly developing my own sense of identity that extended far beyond who I had been led to believe I could be. Without realizing it, I was living a classic 1980s John Hughes coming-of-age film, both artistically and emotionally.

TRACEY WAS A PUNK ROCKER NOW. She was a terrible yet wonderful vision of defiance, dressed in glittering Doc Marten boots, black bondage leggings, an Anti-Pasti T-shirt, and a shaved head. Tracey had changed from the tennis shorts and sneakers she wore last summer to something I had only seen on prime-time TV series like CHiPs or Quincy. But this was no cartoonish, spiky-haired monster terrifying a frivolous sitcom with reckless anarchy and a clamorous soundtrack. No. This was the real deal. Tracey and I went upstairs to her bedroom after the normal merry catch-up, when she began to show me her large record collection next to her turntable system. Rows and rows of seven-inch singles and LPs, all neatly stacked and perfectly cared for, with band names I'd never heard of—the Misfits, Dead Kennedys, Bad Brains, Germs, Naked Raygun, Black Flag, Wire, Minor Threat, GBH, Discharge, the Effigies... too many to name. This was a virtual treasure trove of underground, independent punk rock, which I had never heard of before. THIS WAS THE FIRST DAY OF MY NEW LIFE.

Music was no longer an unachievable feat of sorcery, only accessible to those graced with the godlike ability of Jimi Hendrix or Paul McCartney. All you needed were three chords, an open mind, and a microphone, I realized. And the determination to make it happen on your own. Tracey had planned to take the L downtown that night to watch local Chicago punk band Naked Raygun perform at the Cubby Bear, a dingy club just across the street from Wrigley Field. I was itching to experience this radical lifestyle up close and in the flesh after listening to their song "Surf Combat" that afternoon, but I couldn't imagine Tracey would welcome me along because I looked like a square thirteen-year-old child who'd just tumbled off the back of a public school bus.

After years of watching MTV and staring at KISS and Led Zeppelin posters on my bedroom walls, I mistakenly assumed that bands exclusively performed on big stages with smoke machines and massive displays of lasers and fireworks. That was rock and roll to me. I had no idea that all you needed was four walls and music. My mind was an electrical storm of hazardous premonitions on the train ride into town, envisioning the turmoil and lunacy that lay in that filthy hole-in-the-wall tavern downtown. A truth had been released in me just hours earlier that I couldn't wait to live out. I suddenly associated with something that was unlike anything I had witnessed in my life back home. When we arrived at the Cubby Bear, I was surprised to see a few punks hanging out on the street outside the club door. They weren't the threatening features I'd seen on Tracey's record covers, but they were teenagers like me. Most of them were skinny skaters in jeans, T-shirts, and Converse Chucks, bouncing off the walls with adolescent, frenetic energy, just like me. We strolled up, relieved, and Tracey introduced me to her crew of outsiders. The room was tense as Naked Raygun readied to take the stage, like a bomb about to detonate. The closeness of the gig struck me as soon as the house lights went out. Unlike the posters on my bedroom wall, I was standing shoulder to shoulder with everyone else, barely feet from the small stage, as the vocalist clutched the microphone, ready to count into the first number.

I'D WAITED MY ENTIRE LIFE FOR THIS FEELING OF FREEDOM, AND NOW THAT I'D BEEN BAPTIZED BY SPIT AND SWEAT AND BROKEN GLASS, THERE WAS NO TURNING BACK. I stayed close to the small stage, soaked in the distorted splendor of the music, song after tremendous song. Some believe Naked Raygun to be the most important band in the history of Chicago punk, and their sound resembled a hardcore Dick Dale sort of surf rock. We boarded the train and returned to Evanston with our ears ringing and our hearts reborn. I was eternally changed on that summer day, and I realized that I didn't need fireworks, lasers, or the unachievable proficiency of a virtuoso instrumentalist to become a musician. Naked Raygun's performance had revealed to me the most vital aspect of rock & roll: the raw and imperfect sound of human beings cleansing their innermost voice for all to hear. This was now available to me, and I couldn't wait to return home to Virginia and spread the word to all of my friends in the hopes that they, too, would see the light.

Turns out, Tracey herself was the singer in a punk rock band titled Verboten, and they had previously recorded several original songs and played live shows around Chicago. The four-piece were just kids doing it all themselves, writing and practicing in Tracey's basement, booking their own events, and designing their own T-shirts to sell at their shows. The days of our vacation flew by as I immersed myself in Tracey's music library, studying each album and even discovering a few bands from my hometown in her collection: Minor Threat, Faith, Void, and my personal favorite, a band called Scream, whose Bailey's Crossroads PO box address was only a few miles from my house! Mind. Fucking.

The rest of our trip was spent going to performances, buying music at Wax Trax! records, and hanging around with other punks as I gradually mastered their new language of records and tapes. This underground culture, I saw, was a grassroots network of young music fans like me, blissfully divorced from the mainstream idea of a "career" in music. The long drive back to Virginia felt like a symbolic voyage from the past to the future. I had forgotten something in Chicago. The small child who could never fathom his songs, words, or feelings dwelling deep within the grooves of a dusty black slab of vinyl was long gone. The little boy who was frightened of being teased for being different from all the cool kids was long gone. I was now determined to start my new life as a punk rocker, armed with a Germs record, a Killing Joke T-shirt, and the "Flammable Solid" single I had purchased during the Naked Raygun show. I had finally lost the delicate outer coat of adolescent insecurity and had begun to grow a new skin, one that would form into my genuine personality, and I couldn't wait to display it to the world.

CHAPTER 5
John Bonham Séance

The altar had been prepared. The candles had been lit. The rite had been planned. I knelt silently on the floor in front of the makeshift shrine I had built by hand out of scrap wood and leftover model paint, cleansed my mind of all thoughts, and began to pray. I'm not sure who I was praying to, but I knew exactly what I was praying for. Success. The yellow light from the flickering candles spilled onto the cold concrete floor of my carport, illuminating the symbols I had drawn to summon the spirits that would guide me to my destiny: the John Bonham three-circles logo and the number 606, two emblems that held deep significance in my life. I used my own brand of telepathy to list my deepest wants, hoping that someone, something, somewhere would hear my call and fulfill my prayers in good time. This is known as the "Law of Attraction," which holds that the universe creates for you what your mind focuses on. As a teenager, I knew nothing about this concept, but I knew deep down that anything was possible if I dedicated myself completely to it. My alternatives in life were, at best, limited at this point. With no high school graduation and no family money, I was condemned to live paycheck to paycheck, with music as my driver, which thankfully kept my soul alive. All I could do was fantasize. So I dreamed. But I no longer daydreamed about one day "making it" as a musician. I was determined to compel the unknown to accompany me there.

I used to think of music as merely a sound. Simple nursery songs and radio jingles that I would sing along to aimlessly for pleasure, floating in one ear and out the other. Songs were merely fleeting melodies and rhythms that came and went like the wind, never really capturing my heart, only moving the air I breathed and occupying the time between life's more significant moments. UNTIL THEY BECAME THE AIR I BREATHED ONE DAY. When music got a hold of me, I became hopelessly preoccupied with every facet of its creation, dismissing all other childhood interests. Nothing captivated and excited my intellect more than the writing and arrangement of a song, and I spent every waking hour uncovering this enigma. I didn't refer to the sound as "notes" on paper because I didn't have any formal music training; it developed shapes in my head as I listened carefully to the numerous layers of instruments.

I've only met one other individual in my life who engaged in this bizarre behavior: Kurt Cobain. It's particularly obvious during our MTV Unplugged performance from November 1993 in New York City. At times during the show, you can see Kurt's jaw clenching and moving side to side as if it were a metronome while he strummed his guitar. At the time, I was interested in mysticism and the idea that a person may become one with God or the Absolute, so I was open to examining how that might happen (I was also interested in hallucinogens), but I followed no particular religion in my selfish pursuit. And, while I had a basic understanding of organized religion, I wasn't raised in a religious household and would only go to church with my Episcopal father once a year on Christmas Eve, when we would attend mass at DC's historic St. John's Church. I certainly connected with the spiritual component of it and found the ceremony to be beautiful and uplifting, but that specific set of beliefs had not been ingrained in me since childhood, so it all remained a mystery to me. It wasn't until I was sent to a Catholic high school (for reform, not religion) that I began to study the concept of faith and comprehend what it really meant. MY MOTHER'S LOVE, MY LOVE FOR HER, AND THE LOVE THAT FILLED MY HEART WHEN I PLAYED MUSIC WERE CERTAIN THINGS IN MY LIFE ON WHICH I RELIED UNCONDITIONALLY AND IN WHICH I HAD UNWAVERING FAITH.

So, without the typical structures and norms, I imagined music to be my religion, the record store to be my church, the rock stars to be my saints, and their songs to be my hymns. As I sat in front of my punk rock tabernacle's flickering candles, I reflected on that unconditional faith. It's easy to dismiss it all as coincidence, but as I write this today, with both the three-circles logo and a gothic "606" tattooed into my skin, I have to believe that I manifested my destiny that night, using the Law of Attraction, calling upon the universe, connecting with a higher power, or whatever. I just know that the success I prayed for in my carport that night has come to me today. Or was it that I sold my soul for rock and roll?

PART 2
The Construction

CHAPTER 1
"Anyone seen Skeeter?"

By 1990, my travels with Scream had taken me from Louisiana to Ljubljana, Memphis to Milan, San Francisco to Stockholm, and I had become a seasoned road warrior, no stranger to the occasional crisis or conflict, so having one member missing in action was just another day on the road. What had once been a crash course in how to exist on less than $10 per day in a van had become a familiar, comfortable routine, and I had readily integrated into the life of a traveling vagrant. Since Scream had previously toured Europe before I joined the band, they had already formed a network that welcomed us as family, providing us with places to stay, food to eat, and equipment to use on tour because we couldn't afford to transport our own instruments from home. Most of those pals were musicians as well, and the majority of them lived in squats, abandoned buildings teeming with punks and anarchists, frequently stealing utilities from the city grid to exist. These radical communities were not only intriguing to my young, impressionable mind, but also inspiring, because life in these makeshift communes was stripped down to the most basic human elements, foregoing the trappings of conventional existence (materialism, greed, and social status) in favor of a life of protest, freedom, and the realization that we all need each other to get by. Amsterdam had become our home base for a variety of reasons, some obvious (marijuana), others purely logistical (proximity to Northern Europe). We'd usually save up our money from our menial day jobs at home and fly standby on a Dutch airline called Martinair for $99, arrive at Schiphol international airport, steal a bike the first night, and spend the next few weeks preparing for our tour by making phone calls with a pirated phone card, gathering gear, and renting a van that would become our home for the next few months.

BUT, MORE THAN ANYTHING, I WAS FREE, AND ADVENTURE WAS RIGHT AROUND THE CORNER. When we were all drinking on the pavement in front of our favorite punk rock bar, De Muur, one night in Amsterdam, there was a sudden explosion of activity across the street at the Vrankrijk, one of Holland's most famed squats. An army of skinheads and right-wing fascists had planned an attack on the building, and as they marched up the short street, the Vrankrijk residents braced themselves for fight. Having said that, I was learning about languages and cultures that I would not have learned in school, and the physicality of being in these places improved my sense of the world as a community, which is much smaller than most people imagine. But the border crossings were always entertaining... picture a customs official's delight when a gang of young punks pulled up in a van with Netherlands license plates (large red flag) with guitars and amps (bigger red flag). When I was going down an Amsterdam alleyway with my old friend Marco Pisa, an Italian tattoo artist I met in Bologna when I painted his tattoo shop in exchange for a beautiful branding on my left shoulder, we were approached by two junkies trying to sell us heroin. We weren't fans of heroin (or junkies), so Marco respectfully declined with a firm "Fuck off!" and we continued walking.

But it's possible that Skeeter abandoned us the first time because of our unstable lifestyle. In the spring of 1990, during what would be my final European tour with Scream, he decided that he just couldn't hang and flew home, leaving us stranded on another continent thousands of miles away. We were fortunate to have our dear buddy Guy Pinhas fill in for a few performances, allowing us to continue the tour with just enough money to catch the standby flights back on El Al airlines, but I was beginning to suspect that Skeeter's dedication to the band was not the same as Pete's, Franz's, and mine. We would have done anything to prevent the wheels from falling off.

Skeeter sat me down one day, rolled a massive joint from the paper wrapper of a tampon discovered in the bathroom, and got me so high I couldn't see straight. "All right, we're going to play the same riff for thirty minutes and you're not going to do a single drumroll," he stated. Simple, I reasoned. I sat behind my kit as he started playing his silky bass line, half reggae, part Motown, and I boldly joined in.

It didn't take me 45 seconds to feel the temptation to do a drumroll, but he shook his head and advised me not to, so I kept going with the beat. A minute later, I had the unquenchable want to do a crazy drumroll, almost like a musical Tourette's or hold back a sneeze, but Skeeter merely shook his head. Skeeter was essentially breaking the wild pony, teaching me to respect the simplicity and strength of a rhythm and to stop from unnecessary bluster. I was a completely different drummer after thirty minutes. This was possibly the most important musical instruction I've ever received, and I'll be eternally grateful to him for it.

We didn't pull out the contract and read it in the back of our van until one blazing hot day in Spokane months later, sitting in the parking lot of a Denny's after many performances across the country had been canceled. Because we didn't at this point. The walls were closing in on us, and no matter how hard we tried, it never seemed to be enough. At the very least, there was Los Angeles to look forward to. Los Angeles was always the highlight of every tour, not just for the obvious benefits of a few days in hairspray heaven, but also because we had relatives there: Pete and Franz's sister, Sabrina. Sabrina was the most fun, bubbliest, most gorgeous lady you'd ever seen, having moved from the dull suburbs of Virginia to the glitz of Los Angeles in the late 1980s. We would stay at her apartment whenever we were in town, and she would take us about like an eighties video vixen chaperone, from the brilliant lights of the Sunset Strip to her place of business, the Hollywood Tropicana.

And after the ruthless carnage, we'd return to Sabrina's Laurel Canyon bungalow, which she shared with a few other mud wrestlers, and party all night. The word "slumming" does not spring to mind. Los Angeles interested me almost as much as Europe's millennia of history, but in a far different way. Everything appeared to be... incredible. As much as Washington, DC, could be described as a transitory city, with its social dynamic moving radically with each new government, Los Angeles seemed to change by the minute. People came and went via a revolving door of opportunity and demise, leaving their filth behind for the next wave of visitors to wade through in the goal of becoming the next big thing, as if it were the world's largest Greyhound bus station. There was a sadness that seemed to be covered by excess and overindulgence, making the hangovers that much more difficult to drink away the next morning. Nothing could be more depressing than waking up in a sleeping bag on a mud wrestler's floor, hoping your band member didn't abandon you high and dry. Again.

The days passed, and we managed to subsist as strays thanks to the generosity of our mud-wrestling housemates, who returned home every night emptying their purses full of dollar bills into enormous piles on the living room carpet. Food was sparse, and hunger set in quickly. Our roadie, Barry the Canadian, was receiving Social Security payments to assist keep us from going hungry, but they only lasted so long. I ultimately obtained a job tiling a coffee shop in Costa Mesa to supplement my income, but as time passed, it became clear that we weren't going anywhere anytime soon. Understandably, Barry returned to Canada after understanding that our condition was hopeless. I was beginning to despair and needed even a sliver of relief or rescue from our slowly sinking ship. Our stuff was collecting dust in Sabrina's downstairs garage, but after a week or so, I saw something else collecting dust in that small garage: a black 1985 Honda Rebel 250 cc motorcycle. Each one was no doubt occupied by a rock star, a movie star, a producer or director who had followed their dreams and somehow struck gold, and I wondered how it must feel to achieve that level of success, to live in such comfort, and to know where your next meal was coming from. The gap between this ideal and my reality was so vast, so unfathomable, that it wasn't even worth contemplating. So I simply drove. This was my way out. This was my momentary salvation. This was my lifeboat from the sinking ship in the distance. THEN I HEARD THE FIVE WORDS THAT FOREVER CHANGED MY LIFE: "HAVE YOU EVER HEARD OF NIRVANA?"

Bleach, their debut album, was a milestone record in the underground music scene, fusing metal, punk, and Beatles-esque melody into an eleven-song masterpiece that would go on to revolutionize the landscape of "alternative" music (while also costing $606). It rapidly became one of my favorites and stuck out from the rest of my noisy, heavy punk records because it had SONGS. And that voice... no one else has a voice like it... After a few more days of frustration and famine, I decided to take a chance and phone Nirvana's bassist, Krist, to inquire about the drummer position. I introduced myself and said that a common acquaintance had given me his number, so we talked for a bit until Krist informed me that the post of drummer had already been taken by their good buddy Dan Peters from Mudhoney. So I called Kurt right away and we spoke about music for a long time. We discovered that we had a lot in common musically, from NWA to Neil Young, Black Flag to the Beatles, the Cramps to Creedence Clearwater Revival, and that an audition could be worth pursuing. "Well, if you can make it up here, just let us know," he replied casually in his now-famous drawl. We said our goodbyes, and I was now left with one of the most difficult decisions of my life. I'd felt like a part of a family since the day I joined Scream. Despite my age, Pete, Franz, and Skeeter always regarded me as an equal, and we became close friends, spending practically every day together, tour or no tour. I had spent the most formative years of my life with them, discovering music, discovering the world, and ultimately discovering myself, so moving on and leaving them behind in that sinking ship broke my heart in ways I had never felt before, even more than saying goodbye to my own father when he disowned me for dropping out of high school.

CHAPTER 2
It's a Lifetime Thing

AFTER ALL, IT'S A PERMANENT THING. It was the fall of 1990 in Olympia, Washington, and I had just received my first check from Nirvana as a paid member. It was by far the greatest payout of my professional life up until that point, a whooping $400. This much-needed advance from our newly acquired management business, Gold Mountain, arrived at a time when Nirvana was being courted by every major-label record company known to man in an all-out bidding war, while Kurt and I were physically hungry and living in squalor. Our 114 NE Pear Street apartment was the back unit of a decaying old home built around 1914, with one bedroom, one bathroom, a small living room, and a kitchen the size of a broom closet (ironically located directly across the street from the Washington State lottery facility). It was not Versailles. The word "unclean" doesn't even begin to convey the carnage inside. It transformed the Chelsea Hotel into a Four Seasons.

At the time, I was surviving on a three-for-ninety-nine-cent corn dog special from the Ampm petrol station across the street. The trick was to eat one for breakfast (at noon) and save the other two for a late dinner after rehearsal, which kept me going until hunger pangs set in and I was forced to return to the fluorescent glow of the convenience store lights with another crumpled dollar bill in my hand. This impoverished diet, along with my penchant for playing the drums with every fiber of my thin being five evenings a week, had reduced me to a virtual waiflike marionette, barely filling out the soiled old clothes I kept in a duffel bag on the floor in the corner of the living room. It was enough to send anyone running back to the comforts of their mother's home cooking, but I was 2,786 miles away in Springfield, Virginia. And then I was free. In retrospect, I now see why I went straight to Fred Meyer to get a BB pistol and a Nintendo console. Clearly, I was indulging in childhood luxuries that I had wished for but never received when I was younger. Not to say I was a happy or deprived youngster, but any extra money in my family was kept for more practical things like new shoes or winter jackets (there was once a fifty-dollar minibike, but that's another story).

Soon, our afternoons in Olympia were spent shooting egg cartons from a distance in our old house's backyard and playing Super Mario World till the sun came up (we may or may not have taken a few potshots at the lottery building across the street in the cause of the revolution). Our filthy den had been turned into an adolescent leisure center from hell. This was Versailles to me. However, because I had neither foresight or care for realistic spending, the money quickly ran out, leaving me with just enough money for one more crazy indulgence: a tattoo. Not my first, to be sure. No, that was a self-inflicted masterpiece I created at the age of fourteen with a sewing needle, some thread, and a jug of black ink. After viewing Uli Edel's gritty homemade-tattoo scene in Christiane F., I decided to bedazzle my left forearm in the same DIY method with the insignia of my favorite band at the time, Black Flag. If you've seen the classic Black Flag emblem, you'll recognize it as four thick, black vertical bars in staggered sequence. A tall order for a run-down youngster with his mother's seldom-used sewing kit. I made it through three of the four bars before saying, "Fuuuuck this shit!" and stopping. Not the show-stopping moment I had hoped for, but my heart was suddenly filled with a sense of finality that strangely emboldened me. Something that will last forever.

I accumulated quite a collection of these little blurred diaries all over my body over the years. A little mark here, a little mark there, until I was ultimately graced with the opportunity to get legitimately tattooed by Andrea Ganora, an Italian artist who lived in the famed Amsterdam squat Van Hall. The facility, an old two-story factory, had been taken over and occupied by a small group of punk rockers from all over Europe in late 1987. The frigid, enormous structure was converted into their home by a tight-knit community of friends, complete with a live music club downstairs (where I accidentally made my first live record, SCREAM Live! at Van Hall, in 1988). It became a virtual home base for Scream when I was eighteen. Andrea was the resident tattoo artist, and the majority of Van Hall's residents proudly displayed his work.

My honeymoon on Pear Street soon ended, and I was back to rationing corn dogs and cursing the relentless tapping of the turtle terrarium night after night, head buried in the soiled cushions of that old couch. The lesson has been learned. The season grew dark, and homesickness struck in. I'd left my friends, family, and Virginia behind for... this. The harsh Pacific Northwest winter weather and lack of sunlight just exacerbated the growing sense of sadness, but happily, I still had one thing keeping me from retiring back home: the music. Even though Nirvana may be dysfunctional at times, there was an underlying focus whenever we put our instruments on and the amps started to shine. WE WANTED TO BE THE BEST. Alternatively, as Kurt once told music entrepreneur and giant Donnie Ienner in his New York City high-rise office, "We want to be the biggest band in the world."

Our music was the one thing that kept my mind off the flaws of this new life I'd found, the only thing that made it all worthwhile. Every rehearsal began with a "noise jam," which evolved into an improvisational exercise in dynamics, eventually honing our collective instinct and allowing song structure to happen without needing to be verbally arranged; it would just happen, almost like a flock of blackbirds gracefully ebbs and flows in a hypnotic wave over a country field in the winter. As the long winter gave way to spring, we spent many hours in that makeshift studio working on songs for the album that would become Nevermind. Unlike the other bands I had been in, Nirvana did not play shows frequently for fear of exhausting the local audience, so the majority of our attention was focused on being ready to record once we had decided on a label and producer. Kurt was a wonderfully prolific songwriter, seemingly having a new song idea almost every week, so there was always a sense of forward motion, never feeling trapped or stagnant musically. When I joined Nirvana in September 1990, they had already recorded a fresh batch of songs with their previous drummer, Chad Channing, for their next Sub Pop LP. Butch Vig, a young, up-and-coming producer from Madison, Wisconsin, had recorded songs like "In Bloom," "Imodium" (which became "Breed"), "Lithium," and "Polly" earlier that year.

These compositions, which demonstrated Kurt's ever-evolving songwriting abilities, had a new, mature sense of melody and lyric; they had outgrown the prior material and promised great things to come. Simply put, Nirvana was transforming into Nirvana. This album, when combined with Butch's mega-fucking-rock sound, was responsible for the majority of the industry "buzz" surrounding the band, finally fueling a subsequent feeding frenzy of interest. For most bands, these songs would have been an embarrassment of riches, but Kurt kept writing, and the new songs kept arriving. "Come As You Are," "Drain You," "On a Plain," "Territorial Pissings," and, of course, "Smells Like Teen Spirit." Usually starting with a Kurt riff, Krist Novoselic and I would follow his lead with our seasoned intuition, acting as the engine room to his screaming vision.

The resulting eruption would frequently send chills up my spine, as the undeniable strength of our collective sound became almost too large for that tiny little room. WE WOULDN'T KEEP THESE SONGS A SECRET FOR LONG. They'd quickly sneak up on everyone and catch everyone off guard. It was an easy decision to sign with the David Geffen Company. Following in the footsteps of iconic New York noise heroes Sonic Youth, we hired their manager, John Silva, and thought that any major-label record business gutsy enough to back Sonic Youth's experimental style of no wave would be a safe haven for a band like us. The final piece of the jigsaw was finding a producer who could do justice to these new songs. Kurt's ever-changing sense of melody and lyric is ideal. Butch Vig was eventually our man. To begin with, there is no simpler hang than a Butch Vig hang. The adjective "chill" only scratches the surface of his Midwest Zen disposition. Just. Fucking. Cool.

With its grungy, no-nonsense, analog look and a history of iconic records, it seemed the right fit. Not to mention that it was closer to the Geffen offices in Hollywood, and I'm quite sure they wanted to keep an eye on us to make sure we weren't pulling another great rock and roll fraud a la the Sex Pistols (which we did consider at one point). It's hard to blame them. The danger element was perhaps a notch higher than with our label partners Edie Brickell & New Bohemians, but they had no idea we were serious. We began final preparations for our thousand-mile journey down to Los Angeles once the dates were finally set (May 2-19). We were ready to go after a few more practices and a few more boom box recordings of new song ideas. So, we're almost there. We needed money for gas. We hurriedly booked a last-minute concert at the OK Hotel, a small bar in downtown Seattle, hoping to make enough money to fill our tanks and get us to Sound City without breaking down on the side of the road.

It was April 17, 1991, and the small room was thankfully packed with sweaty kids eager to hear Nirvana's greatest hits. "School," "Negative Creep," "About a Girl," and "Floyd the Barber" were all known to Nirvana's first album, Bleach, so we performed them with our usual wild abandon, pounding our instruments to within an inch of their lives while the crowd shouted every word. It was virtually transcendent, just like every other Nirvana show I'd seen. I knew deep down that I wouldn't be returning as Kurt and I packed the ancient Datsun for the trek to Los Angeles. With my duffel bag slung over my shoulder, I took one final look at the tiny room I had called home for the past seven months, attempting to imprint every detail in my mind so that I would never forget the memories or meaning of this place in my life. To ensure that whatever came after these days was constructed here. And as I closed the door to go, my heart swelled with a sense of finality, like a needle stabbing into your skin, leaving fuzzy memories of events that will never fade. A small mark here, a small mark there, indelible recollections of times gone by. AFTER ALL, IT'S A PERMANENT THING.

CHAPTER 3
We were surrounded, with no way out.

Hello and welcome to the fall of 1991. Trees nightclub in Dallas' Deep Ellum district was just another stop on the North American part of our "Nevermind" tour, which had a simplified agenda of thirty rigorous gigs in forty days. This relatively new club, with a maximum capacity of roughly 600 people, was comparable to most of the other venues booked for that tour: crowded, a low stage, minimal PA and lights, and a small dressing room in the back to prepare for (and recuperate from) another cathartic performance. In retrospect, Trees was one of the larger rooms booked for us on that trip, because we were more accustomed to playing much smaller places like the Moon in New Haven, Connecticut, where we had squeezed 100 people into its tiny, low-ceilinged room just a few weeks before, or J.C. Dobbs in Philadelphia, which was sold out with 125 paying customers a few days later, or even the 9:30 Club in DC, where we had surely exceeded their official capacity.

A far cry from my days in Scream, when we either slept in the van, crashed at the house of some random stranger we met at the gig, or sometimes resorted to sleeping bags spread out on the beer-soaked stage we had just rocked hours before for a good night's sleep (yes, I have cuddled up to my drum set on numerous occasions). There was also a significant wage increase. Actually, double! The difference between my $7.50-per-day Scream per diem and Nirvana's $15 per diem made me feel rich beyond my wildest dreams. Not that I was ready to put a down payment on a Hamptons mansion just yet, but I had finally progressed from generic smokes to authentic Marlboros, and that made me feel like a fucking king. At twenty-two, I had finally attained a long-awaited life milestone: I was touring the world comfortably with a band that was selling out concert after performance to amazing reviews and quickly gaining recognition. Perhaps a little too hastily.

Nirvana's Nevermind was released on September 24, 1991, just a few days after the first gig of the tour, and I noticed a difference within a week. Not only in the number of people that came to the shows, but also in the type of people who came. They were no longer made up of Sub Pop fans and college radio junkies who had come to hear their favorite songs from the band's first album, Bleach; there was an influx of folks who seemed a little more... mainstream. In my appearance as the keynote speaker at the South by Southwest music festival in 2013, I addressed this ethical crossroads: What is the next step? Where do you go as an artist nurtured in the ethically suffocating punk rock underground, conditioned to reject conformity and defy all corporate influence and expectation? How do you deal with such success? How do you define success now? Is it still a pleasure to play a song from start to finish without making a mistake? Is it still the discovery of a new chord or scale that makes you forget about your problems? How do you deal with the transition from "us" to "them"?

I sensed a tug of battle within myself. I had discovered rock and roll on the AM radio in my mother's car as a child, singing along to 1970s Top 40 songs, but I was now ambivalent about having my own Top 40 hit. My music-loving heart had become a confused and callused lump within my jaded chest after years of being a "punk rocker," renouncing mainstream music, yelling "sellout" to any band that moved even marginally toward mainstream success. One issue was that we were now attracting the same individuals who used to kick our asses in high school for being different, calling us "faggots" and "queers" because of the clothes we wore and music we listened to. Our fanbase was evolving, with macho monster-truck homophobes and meathead jokes whose lives revolved around beer and football. We had always been the odd ones out. We'd always been the oddballs. We were not among them. So, how did they come to be one of us? Then there was the video.

The "Smells Like Teen Spirit" video premiered on MTV's 120 Minutes on September 29, just a few days after the release of our album. 120 Minutes, a late-night alternative music program, was regarded as the launch pad for many underground bands' careers, displaying some of our heroes such as the Pixies, Sonic Youth, Dinosaur Jr., and Hüsker Dü. It was an honor for a band like ours to be recognized among such illustrious companies. It was a watershed moment for us, both personally and professionally, and to deny that we were overjoyed would be a lie. We all sat in our hotel rooms on a night off between our New York City and Pittsburgh gigs, waiting for our film to be aired for the first time ever. On that tour, Kurt and I had a room, and I recall laying across from each other in our twin beds with the television on, watching movies by Morrissey, the Wonder Stuff, and Transvision Vamp for what seemed like an eternity; the suspense grew unbearable with each passing second. The Damned, the Red Hot Chili Peppers, Nine Inch Nails, video after video, till... First, we shot a brief promo backstage at the Reading Festival in England a month prior, when we uncomfortably exclaimed, "You're watching 120 Minutes!" from the catering tent behind the stage, Kurt's arm still bandaged in a sling from maniacally leaping into my drum set that day. I screamed from my stiff Best Western bed, overwhelmed with excitement and the sensation of tripping on too much acid (not mutually exclusive). Oh my God! I pondered.

WE WERE ALL OBVIOUSLY CONNECTED TO THIS SENTIMENT, BUT WE COULDN'T PREDICT THAT AN ENTIRE GENERATION WOULD FEEL THE SAME. The tape was first only shown at night because MTV thought it too contentious for prime-time viewing, but it quickly made its way into the regular rotation. Once there, it spread like wildfire and burned our entire world to the ground. This is typical for a band like us. The world outside of our little bubble was changing quickly: autographs and radio interviews, packed arenas, and repeated near-riots. We had to abandon the stage at our Mississippi Nights show in St. Louis just days before our show at Trees because the crowd rushed the stage, prompted by Kurt's frustration with local security being too rough with the fans, a common occurrence for venues unfamiliar with slam dancing and stage diving.

We had no idea what to anticipate by the time we arrived in Dallas. But there was an electricity in the air that night, amplified by an exceptionally swampy humidity that added to the tension in the room, like a short fuse on a homemade bomb. The crowd was already spilling over the floor monitors and onto Kurt's and Krist's guitar pedals as we came onstage to play, and the band hadn't even hit a single note. The place went insane, as the manic, raw energy of the audience grew tremendously minute by minute. By the time we got to "School," six songs into the set, the crowds on stage had become so dangerous that Kurt couldn't sing into the microphone without getting kicked in the face and crashing into his teeth. I could sense his annoyance, and I was all too aware of what happened when Kurt became furious. SOMETHING WAS DESTRUCTING. I knew it was coming, whether it was his guitar, his amp, or my drums. The countdown started... Four songs later, following a raucous, technically challenging performance of our generally peaceful acoustic tune "Polly," Kurt snapped. Turning to his left, he removed his guitar and began chopping at the monitor engineer's soundboard, sending buttons, knobs, and shrapnel flying across the stage. Kurt had had his fill. Not just of this show, but of everything that had brought us here. This is not something that most performers think about, but then again, we weren't like most performers. What was happening to us had no rulebook. The only way to survive in the Wild West was to follow the light at the end of each long, dark tunnel. My days in Scream had been wild, sleeping in squats, being pursued by skinheads and junkies through dark alleyways, never knowing where my next food would come from, but nothing compared to this. This was perilous.

Nonetheless, we soldiered on, playing while the monitor engineer jokingly placed a wood pallet over his mixing desk in dread of another thrashing. Nothing could save him at this point. This speeding train had already gone off the rails, crashing through everyone and everything in its path. The craziness continued as we began another cover, Shocking Blue's "Love Buzz" (the first Nirvana hit). Body after body fell to the stage, the room heating up with every distorted chord, every inch of skin drenched in the sweat of 600 strangers. Kurt dived into the mob, guitar in hand, and soloed while crowd-surfing atop the gyrating mass of greasy hair and tattooed limbs after the second chorus of the song. As he tumbled back to the platform, flailing in a frenzied, spasmodic dance, he collided with a massive security guard who had been stationed there to keep the kids offstage. After finishing the concert with our quickest, most punk-rock-sounding song, "Territorial Pissings," we eventually laid our instruments down and went to the dressing room, rather frightened by the evening's unusual turn of events. We were used to commotion and disarray, but this was different. This was not enjoyable. This was quite dark. At the very least, it was over. We all made it through another day, and our traveling circus continued on to the next city. With twelve days remaining on the journey, the wheels may still fall off, but at least we were heading in the correct direction: home. We were totally weary, both mentally and physically, by the time we returned to Seattle for our final homecoming gig on Halloween. We had made our mark and returned with scars to show it. We went from three disheveled young guys with little to lose to three disheveled young men with a gold record in forty days. Our worlds had now been eternally altered, as had yours. This was only the beginning. WE WERE ESCAPED. AND THERE WAS NO EXIT.

CHAPTER 4
The Distinction

1992 dawned with a debilitating, well-deserved hangover as I awoke in a sloppy hotel room the night before after spending New Year's Eve with the Red Hot Chili Peppers, Nirvana, Pearl Jam, and sixteen thousand other people at San Francisco's Cow Palace. Nirvana had ended our stormy, historic year with a brief West Coast tour of venues, all packed to the rafters with thousands of young punks eager to see these three up-and-coming bands in what was soon becoming a musical revolution. Looking out from the stage every night, it was evident that a profound cultural revolution was on the way, owing to the enthusiasm and aesthetic of the people who sang along to every word at deafening volume. This was no longer just the sound of the underground or late-night college radio; it was a fucking battering ram to the gates of mainstream popular culture, and our three bands were leading the charge.

Aside from the shifting tides of the musical scene, life from my tiny West Seattle bedroom was in upheaval, with each day bringing a new, absurd development in Nirvana's crazy little world. I clung to the rickety carnival ride that had once been our tiny group as it spun faster and faster, intensifying our unforeseen endeavor to alter the world, but it was futile. It was out of our hands at this point, and no matter how hard we tried, we couldn't stop it. The album we made in under twelve days at that run-down old facility in Los Angeles called

Sound City was now selling 300,000 copies per week. And the news that we had dethroned Michael Jackson at the top of the Billboard album rankings arrived on the same day that we were to appear on Saturday Night Live for the first time, January 11, 1992. This was my education as a young musician, a master class in live performance by some of the world's most cutting-edge performers. But if there was one performance that stood out from the rest and changed the trajectory of my life, it was the B-52s performing their single "Rock Lobster" in 1980.

THESE THREE MINUTES WERE NOT JUST A BAND PLAYING A SONG, BUT A RALLYING CRY TO ALL PEOPLE SUFFOCATING IN CONVENTIONALITY, AFRAID TO LET THEIR FREAK FLAG FLY, WHO WANTED TO CELEBRATE ALL OF LIFE'S BEAUTIFUL ECCENTRICITIES. My thoughts weren't quite this intricate when I was ten years old; I know that now. Even still, their pleasure in their oddness made me feel empowered. I knew I wanted to break free as I watched them dance their mess around in a goofy, frantic blur. I no longer desired to conform to the standard. Like the B-52s, I wanted to break away from the herd and live a life apart from the crowd. There comes a time in every child's life when freedom and individuality collide, directing you in the right direction, and this was mine. I'd be an outcast with a guitar who enjoyed both music and comedy. So there you have it. Kurt began playing the intro to "Smells Like Teen Spirit," and my life flashed before my eyes, despite the fact that I'd played it every night in crowded theaters all around the world by then. This was where the B-52s had been stationed. Devo had been standing here. This was the spot where David Bowie had stood. Every living star, from Bob Dylan to Mick Jagger, had stood on this stage to perform their songs for millions of young musicians like myself, who had stayed up long past their bedtime to see their heroes perform the songs that had changed their lives. I wanted to pass out. I felt like puking. I wanted to run away. But I blasted that drum start with everything I had and... broke a stick. Fuck.

In January 1991, I was in Los Angeles visiting a buddy when I learned Kurt was using heroin. I had never met anyone who had used heroin and understood very little about it, so I was taken aback. I'd only been in the band for three months and was living in a little flat with Kurt, and perhaps naively, I didn't think he'd do something like that. To me, heroin was a nasty street narcotic, only used by prostitutes and junkies in downtown alleyways, not by gentle, kind, loving artists with the world at their feet. I'd read fantastical stories of great rock artists getting strung out in innumerable rock bios that practically celebrated that conduct as some sort of badge of honor, but I never believed it would become a part of my world. Washington, DC was not always a heroin hotspot. Seattle, on the other hand, was known as the heroin capital of the world.

I FINALLY FELT THE DEPARTURE. Those who did and those who did not participated. That difference widened as our world expanded. Nirvana consisted of three distinct persons, each with his own quirks and peculiarities that contributed to the distinct sound we generated when we strapped on our instruments, but outside of the music, we lived our own lives, each extremely different from the others. Kurt's frailty struck me as we shot the video, and I was frightened not only for his health but also for the tour we were about to embark on, which would take us to the other side of the earth, far from the people we loved and needed the most. I couldn't see how we'd make it through another crazy schedule of show after show, airport after airport, and hotel after hotel, especially considering his health, but we did.

The brilliant sun of Australia's summer and our Aussie hosts' even sunnier temperament were a wonderful and much-needed relief from the dreary winter we had left behind back home. It was the perfect spot to be at the perfect time, and for a little minute, our wheels appeared to be back on track. I had been throughout North America and Europe, but I had no idea what to anticipate from this side of the planet, and I took to it like a fly to barbecue. If Australia was a different hemisphere, Japan was a different planet. Every part of existence was a major culture shock. I felt like I was a million miles away from home. And I enjoyed it. We'd never seen anything like Japan, and they'd never seen anything like us either. We played our first gig in Osaka at a facility that looked more like the Kennedy Center than the customary beer-stained, bleach-scrubbed dive pubs where we started. This motivated us to play even harder that night, hoping to elicit a riotous reaction by storming through the songs like never before, and as I looked out from behind my drum set, I could see the audience itching to break out, scream, burst, and fly their own freak flags. Every few songs, a fan would snap and rush to the stage only to be stopped by a pair of white gloves and removed from the show. It was us versus them, I reasoned. I pushed myself ever harder.

We knew exactly what to do at the end of the night... bash the heck out of our equipment (a signature technique by now). Kurt, Krist, and I completely trashed our gear in front of the audience, like three children having a tantrum after being told "No dessert" by Mom and Dad. Instead, we served dessert to that crowd. We exited the stage in a heap of drums, overturned amps, and shrieking feedback, and I was approached by a young Japanese man who was shaking like a leaf and crying. Before returning home, we made one last stop in Hawaii for a gig at Pink's Garage, a little club in Honolulu that was way too small for the band, which was now at the height of its success. Knowing that this was the final show of our tour before a long break at home, I planned to stay for a week afterward, renting a ridiculous ocean-blue Mazda Miata convertible and buzzing around from beach to beach like an annoying tourist (which I was), reaping the benefits of the most insane year of my entire life.

I had never held a credit card, an ATM card, or even a bank account with more than a hundred dollars (thank you, Grandma), so this was a game changer for me at the age of twenty-three. For the previous four years, I had survived on meager per diems that would vanish by the end of each day, squandered on cigarettes, junk food, and alcohol. It was all too nice to be true! Despite the fact that the band had sold well over a million records, I had yet to spend a penny of the money I had gained, naïve to how much it might be. I was about to discover the truth.

As they say, the rest is history. Tan, nourished, and content, I went right back to Virginia after my week on Fantasy Island with Mr Roarke and Tattoo, my first "vacation" since I was a youngster, but with this newfound financial freedom came increased obligations. The unthinkable has finally occurred. I was wealthy. There could be solace after a lifetime of watching my mother juggle many jobs and count every dime. I stayed pretty frugal, oblivious to the immensity of what was to come, as my father (who had recovered from the disowning) soon reminded me, "You know this isn't going to last, right? As was our custom, we dispersed in various directions. Krist returned to Seattle and purchased a warm, cozy home in the Green Lake neighborhood to the north of the city. Kurt moved to Los Angeles and found a charming modest flat in an old Hollywood building. I bought a house in Corolla, North Carolina, only blocks from the ocean, because I wasn't ready to commit to living full-time in Seattle. The Outer Banks, only a few hours from Northern Virginia, was the ideal place for me to invest in real estate, not only because of its raw natural beauty, with high dunes and wild horses running along the wide beaches, but also because of its proximity to home, allowing me to share my profits with my mother and sister. BUT "IDLE HANDS ARE THE DEVIL'S PLAYGROUND," I'VE BEEN TOLD.

As we all settled into our new lifestyles, the schism reappeared. We were no longer crammed together in tight vehicles or shared hotel rooms for months on end, and we were finally free to live the life we had always imagined, for better or worse. We had witnessed the world transform around us, a swirl of flashbulbs and near-riots at every turn, but now that the hurricane of lunacy had passed, we were free to create our own realities however we saw fit. As the band's anonymous drummer, I was fortunate to go through life almost unnoticed, rarely stopped in public, and typically just asked, "Are you Dave Navarro?" It was almost as if I were on the outside looking in, seeing this all unfold from afar, enjoying the perks of "making it" without having to answer for it. With nothing but time until Nirvana's next tour, I bounced from surfing in North Carolina to revisiting my old DC haunts with lifelong friends, to recording my primitive songs in Barrett Jones' basement in Seattle, to flying down to L.A. to reconnect with my old friends Pete and Franz from Scream, who had stayed there since the day I left to join Nirvana, starting new lives (and a new band, Wool) after Scream's demise.

My excitement was tinged with dread as we approached the mansion on Cielo Drive, realizing that the sick fascination I'd always felt with this house was going to be met with the unsettling reality of stepping within its cursed walls. We rang the gatebell, drove into the driveway, stepped out of the car, and there it was, precisely as it had been in every crime scene photo I had ever placed my youthful, inquisitive eyes on. My spine was chilled. Nine Inch Nails were setting a new standard in this venue. I hadn't met Nine Inch Nails, but I had seen them perform live. My teenage soundtrack included Throbbing Gristle, Psychic TV, Einstürzende Neubauten, and Current 93, among others. I really liked NIN's first album, Pretty Hate Machine. With the band's violent electro-tension and dark lyrical themes, it was only natural that they would record their second album at the Manson mansion. After a time, the house's pervasive mood clearly threw a pall over the spirit of the environment, one with which I couldn't connect or jibe at all. I was all too familiar with the feeling of gloom, fragility, and agony, so I went to the pool not only to cool down, but also to wash away the feeling I had standing in that living room.

The darker side of music was always something I was sonically drawn to, but I realized it wasn't who I was as a person. To me, music has always signified brightness and vitality. Even joy. I wanted to celebrate finding a way out of the tunnel. I wanted to wave my freak flag. I didn't want to go into hiding. The rest of my days in LA were spent driving around in a rented white Volkswagen Cabriolet convertible (yes, I had a thing for convertibles at the time), swimming in strangers' pools, jamming with friends, and calling the airlines every few days to change my return ticket to Seattle, extending my stay on Pete's scorching-hot floor for a little more summer and a little more distance before returning to the gray skies up north. I knew nothing about the convoluted web of busy freeways that crisscrossed the vast city, so I began speeding through the Valley at unsafe speeds, hoping to be heading in the general direction of at least one access ramp. I noticed one only meters ahead of me as I screamed around a corner, so I twisted the wheel to the right as hard as I could and... BAM! I took a cab back to Pete's house with a black eye and my tail between my legs for another week's stay, having utterly damaged a perfectly nice Cabriolet convertible that cost only $12 a day. The extra week in Los Angeles allowed me to rest my black eye while simultaneously planning my next steps.

The world had finally heard about Nirvana. We were the out-of-the-ordinary freaks that the entire world was suddenly watching. Could we make it? Kurt was discovered to be at a recovery facility in Los Angeles. I was concerned, but not shocked. This was a good sign for me. While I was reuniting with old acquaintances on the other side of town, perhaps he was finding some light and calm of his own. I had never met anyone who had gone to rehab, so I assumed it was a quick fix, like an appendectomy or having your tonsils removed. Aside from my father's issues with alcohol, I had no idea what addiction was like. To be sure, I was unaware of Kurt's depths. I hadn't realized that the mending required to break free from the grips of this type of illness takes a lifetime—if you can hold on and stay out of the abyss.

THERE WAS STILL SO MUCH TO BE EXCITED ABOUT. WE'D ONLY JUST STARTED.

PART 3
Phenomena

CHAPTER 1
The Nevermind Phenomenon

So, why did Chad Channing exit through the same revolving door that brought Dave into Nirvana? In reality, things did not go precisely as planned. The Melvins' Dale Crover (again) and Mudhoney's Dan Peters were utilized as musical band-aids to keep the grueling gig schedule going, implying that the split was less than planned. Kurt is believed to have inadvertently revealed his replacement to Peters on the local KAOS radio station. In Michael Azerrad's Come As You Are, the officially sanctioned Nirvana biography, Chad expressed a desire to "be a part of what was going on... it was then I realized that it really is Kurt's show, and that what he says goes and that's it, no questions asked." The retiring drummer, who could also play violin, bass, and guitar, had begun to have songwriting ambitions, which was plainly a no-no in a band that was a dictatorship in that regard. (Kurt had mocked Channing for listening to 'elfin' music... you just kind of shudder because it's so silly and lame.') 'I'm really delighted he did, because I adore that song!' remarked Kurt of his temporary substitute Peters, who played on 'Silver' and, according to Kurt, helped create it. He also praised Peters as 'rhythmically adept,' but their match 'wasn't quite ideal.'

In July 1990, Peters was ready to go for a tour with Mudhoney, and the trio happened to be in Reciprocal Studios, where Tad was recording. "We walked in there half an hour after they finished, used their equipment, and recorded the song ('Sliver').' Krist was ecstatic at the unexpected. 'We jumped straight in there and recorded it... the song came together really well.' The first meeting between Cobain and Grohl, Nirvana's new and likely short-lived drummer, was a disaster, and the second would be even worse. The two first laid eyes on each other at a party in Olympia where Kurt's then-girlfriend, Tobi Vail, was one of the performers. Several months passed before Grohl and Cobain reconnected, this time in Seattle, at the Sea-Tac venue where Scream was performing. The outgoing Grohl offered Kurt an apple, but he declined because 'it will make my teeth bleed!' Kurt said that they'd been seeking for someone to sing harmonies for a while, citing Chad Channing's jazzy style: 'He'd switch to something heavier with us, but he couldn't do it naturally.'

Dave first met Nirvana while staying at Krist and Shelli Novoselic's residence in Tacoma. He subsequently moved in with Kurt at his Olympia apartment for eight months, during which time he worked hard to coax the turtle-loving guitarist out of his shell. Despite this, 'we would sit in this tiny shoebox flat for eight hours at a time without uttering a word.' While Dave Grohl's post-Nirvana poetry has been scrutinized for references to his flatmate-turned-bandmate, he would not admit to any such inspiration until 2005. The song, 'Friend of a Friend' from the In Your Honor double album, was written during the era before the band made it, and related to someone who needed a 'silent room / with a lock to keep him in' and who had never been in love 'but knows just what love is'. Even the phrase 'he says nevermind' appears in the lyrics. Grohl celebrated the release of the song by recounting those chilly, lonely days in an interview with Independent journalist Craig McLean. '

The first show of what would become the canonical Nirvana lineup took place on October 11, 1990, at Olympia's tiny North Shore Surf Club. Grohl says, "The venue was down the street from where Kurt and I lived." 'After sound-checking, I went to get some food. There was a line around the block when I returned. "Mother, there's at least 200 people in line!" I called my mother. I was astounded. The band regularly outnumbered the audience in Scream.' Grohl, whose pre-gig anxieties are notorious in the music industry, was no less apprehensive when he eventually took the stage. 'I didn't know anyone in the audience or in the band. I was entirely alone. That hour on stage was the only thing that mattered. That's all I was thinking about.' They kept blowing the power, but the audience reaction made up for it. Musically, Dave was influenced by DRI, Corrosion of Conformity, Motörhead, and Slayer, elements that resurfaced in his Probot project over a decade later.

Kurt and Krist had a love of the creative, extreme Swiss heavy metal band Celtic Frost, but they also shared other interests. 'No one realizes that the creators of Nevermind were huge fans of Flipper and the Butthole Surfers,' Dave says. 'That was the music we grew up with, and while it didn't always come through in Nirvana's music, the spirit was there. We all grew up with the same music. It was one of my first interactions with Kurt. We all enjoyed the same music, from Celtic Frost to Neil Young to Public Enemy.' That wasn't entirely correct. Dave returned to Europe for the second time as a working musician just a month after joining Nirvana for a UK tour with L7. No one knew what name would be printed on the work permit the day before they arrived. Perhaps they intended to scribble the name of the band's fourth drummer in a year in pencil in case another change occurred.

Dave was presumably still feeling his way through the set at this point, and Kurt was reportedly seen helping him through the songs before the final takes. Despite this, the versions of 'Molly's Lips' and 'Son of a Gun' were released on the Incesticide compilation. Typically, the two tracks just cited were not even Nirvana songs, but cover versions of songs by the Vaselines, a little-known Scottish group. They were formed in 1987 in Edinburgh by singer/guitarists Eugene Kelly and Frances McKee, who were heavily influenced by the Velvet Underground. Peel had a well-deserved reputation for giving airtime to ground-breaking acts, having single-handedly broken the Ramones in 1976, before punk took off in the UK. He had already broadcast a session by the Chad Channing lineup in late 1989, and this session, broadcast in early November, was the second of four BBC recordings they recorded - three for John Peel, one for Mark Goodier. Despite the fact that they were supposedly promoting a single, 'Sliver,' produced before Dave joined the band, its absence from the Peel Session was an indicator of the priority that assignment was given. It was Nirvana's relationship with the UK music press that would prove more important in the months and years to come Ironically, Alex Macleod, the local tour manager, had handled Scream's European tour; though he and Dave didn't get along at that time, they managed to coexist pretty peacefully.

The Sub Pop label was still reeling from cash-flow issues, so with Nirvana attracting press attention like flies around garbage, a label change was plainly in the works. Many A&R executives attended the UK gigs, anxious to rule over one of the world's top unsigned acts After returning from Britain, the big record companies' courtship of Nirvana became an entertaining scenario. Guns N'Roses had taken this aspect of their artistic lives to ludicrous extremes a few years ago since they couldn't afford to feed themselves; Nirvana reacted similarly. Kurt cheerfully ate the pricey meal served, much to the disadvantage of the discourse, whilst Krist was inclined to have a little fun. David Geffen, the guy behind the mega-platinum success of bands ranging from the Eagles to Guns N'Roses, was one of the band's most ardent pursuers. He sought to find a third world-beater to rank with his prior hits and kick off the label with a boom after launching a new imprint, DGC, to corner the alternative rock market They already had Sonic Youth, but Nirvana may be far greater.

Kurt was pleased on two counts: his allegiance to Sub Pop might not have allowed him to sever the links so completely (in fact Mudhoney stayed with the label for another album), but he could now deliver his music to a much bigger prospective audience. He may not have liked Guns N'Roses (the two bands memorably clashed backstage at the 1992 MTV Video Music Awards), but he was clearly fascinated by the size of their crowds. When the band signed with Geffen in January 1991, they agreed to be paid until the advance of $287,000 was received. However, because they'd partnered with Sonic Youth's management business, Gold Mountain, who had plenty of acumen, their contract favored a greater royalty rate above the largest potential advance - a foresighted strategy.

The Nevermind recordings, for which Dave had specially ordered a loud brass snare drum called "the Terminator," took place at Sound City Studios in Van Nuys, California, in May and June 1991. The recording session was unhurried. Krist says that they slept all day, then laid on the couch and played pinball,' while Kurt recalls that 'we downed a lot of hypodermic cough syrup and Jack Daniels, and simply lounged in the recreation section of the studio for days on end, penning down a few lyrics here and there.' 'Teen Spirit' did the trick, and 'Come As You Are' was the follow-up. Behind the scenes, though, Kurt's health was generating anxiety. He suffered from chronic stomach symptoms that were never adequately diagnosed, preventing Nirvana from traveling in support of Nevermind (then at number one). The band's behavior was so chaotic that they were booted out of the album launch party in a Seattle bar, which devolved into a food fight. Butch Vig, who had recently finished the Smashing Pumpkins' Gish, was chosen over Don Dixon and Scott Litt, both of whom had produced REM, and David Briggs, who had produced several great Neil Young albums. Vig, who would later go on to become a drummer with the band Garbage, had seen Nirvana previously, but never with new member Dave Grohl. He was soon persuaded.

Nirvana went on tour with Sonic Youth in the summer of 1991, giving Dave his first taste of European festivals. And he had a good time because of his label buddies. 'Every day, we were lucky enough to witness Sonic Youth perform all of their best songs - at the time, 'Kool Thing,' 'Schizophrenia,' etc. Every day, out in the rain, it was a virtual greatest hits compilation. It was fantastic. I believe the first was the Pukkelpop phenomenon in Belgium. We went on at 11 a.m., with the Ramones as the opening act. It was fantastic.' Dave supposedly banged the drums so hard during the recording of Nevermind that the heads had to be replaced every other song. Comparisons between the finished recordings and the demos cut at

Smart studios with Chad Channing reveal astonishingly little difference save for the intensity with which the parts are played. Dave confesses that his predecessor did some "really cool stuff," despite not being the most solid or reliable sticksman. Butch Vig, the band's producer, agreed with Cobain and Novoselic that the band had found their ideal drummer: 'Grohl is tremendously loud and rock solid. 'One of the most talented drummers I've ever worked with.' 'I'm a drummer, so I'm quite sensitive about drum sounds,' Vig remarked of the Sound City facilities in Van Nuys, California, where Nevermind was recorded. The studio featured a large tracking room that would allow us to produce a solid live drum sound.' The thunderous drumming on 'Smells Like Teen Spirit' was inspired by a fight between Grohl and Cobain. 'For whatever reason, Kurt really got on Dave's case and pissed him off,' says Vig. Grohl's enraged flailing fueled the track. Cobain, who was a bit of a drummer himself, had firm views about what he wanted, which might be a hindrance to advancement.

Dave's all-or-nothing approach hampered the recording of the almost folky 'Something in the Way,' the album's most recently composed song and official closer. Bass and drums were added to Cobain's soft acoustic guitar and vocal performance, although Dave, in the words of producer Vig, had to be reminded to 'play weak' all the time. Vig stated, 'It almost killed him to tap his way through.' Nevermind's entrance in the rock world in September 1991 was like a hurricane. Some journalists thought Nirvana were the grunge figureheads, while others thought Nevermind transcended the genre. In terms of fashion, the retail industry pounced on Cobain's "non-image," and plaid work shirts, striped jumpers, and torn trousers suddenly flooded the high streets as a new "grunge look." Cobain seemed to draw more column inches as the 'star du jour' as he tried to defy the trend with granddad cardigans and even cross-dressing. It was one big chuckle for Dave Grohl, who still wore his shoulder-length hair. 'We were defrauding the entire world. How could anyone think we deserved to be such a big band... Have you seen us in person? It was amusing. MTV, magazines, and critics' choices were all irrelevant. All that mattered was that the three of us were making music. And I don't believe we wrote a single poor song. Everything we did together was absolutely awesome.'

Despite the label move, Dave expected the upcoming album to be "like another successful independent record vibe." I didn't expect it to be that different from Bleach - simply a step up.' Events suggested he got it completely wrong. Nevermind had a very spectacular rise, debuting at Number 144 in the US charts on its September 1991 release. The next week, it climbed to 109, then 65, and finally 35, to enter the all-important Top 50. Three weeks later, it was at Number Four, aided by MTV's strong play of first single 'Smells Like Teen Spirit,' about which alt.country artist Ryan Adams famously said: 'If you're in a bar and it comes on, if you don't air guitar by accident, you're thinking about it.'

It reached the top of the US chart in January 1992 (the three million milestone was attained when it hit Number One), and it would alternate with country musician Garth Brooks for several weeks afterwards. As if that weren't enough, latecomers were now eagerly rediscovering Nirvana's Sub Pop past: Bleach was suddenly selling at a rate of 70,000 copies per month. Nevermind was first played on British radio by DJs Mark Goodier and John Peel, but Geffen's radio pluggers were eager to get 'Teen Spirit' on daytime radio. Despite Nirvana playing unexceptional UK shows and canceling others, both the single and the album reached Number Seven. The 'Lithium' single was released ahead of their second Reading festival performance in August 1992, with the album having gone platinum the previous month with the sale of the 300,000th UK copy. With the lengthy roadwork success demanded, Nirvana would struggle to find the time and inspiration to create a follow-up of the same magnificent dimensions. And Kurt was never going to make a carbon duplicate of Nevermind in the first place.

The final show was a Hallowe'en homecoming party at the Paramount Theatre in Seattle, alongside Mudhoney and Bikini Kill. They were public property by then, though at least one survivor recalls remarkably little. 'It's really difficult to recall everything,' Grohl acknowledges. 'I wish I'd kept a diary. I wish I had taken photos. I was as perplexed then as I am today about the whole thing.' The set list stayed consistent throughout, beginning with 'Aneurysm,' the US B-side to 'Teen Spirit,' and finishing with 1989 EP track

'Blew,' which Novoselic described as a 'freak-out at the end when things would get broken up.' Dave and Kurt completely destroyed the former's old drum equipment in an attempt to persuade the record company to buy him a new one, according to the Metro in Chicago. Dave realized they'd made it when, exactly 15 months after his first Nirvana show, he performed in front of the cameras of Saturday Night Live on January 11, 1992. The US television institution was not only a part of his life, but it was also a small-town boy's first introduction to punk. He remembered seeing Devo and the B-52s on the show, so being on it 12 years later was "crazy... I felt like I was going to faint." That week, I was also number one on the charts...' The album's smashing opening track, 'Smells Like Teen Spirit,' had been released a fortnight earlier and was already tearing up the world's singles list like a particularly furious chainsaw. The guitar riff, which was first performed solo before being repeated as the band crashed in behind it, had roughly the same effect.

If Grohl's work with Nirvana inspired and defined a generation of drummers, it's the stark simplicity of Nevermind that he's rightfully most proud of. 'Our objective was to write something so simple, almost infantile; simple rhythms and patterns - the most direct songwriting.'The albums that first got me interested in drumming as a kid featured simple rhythms, like the Beatles or AC/DC, or even the drums on disco recordings. I could hear the kick and the snare, and it was so easy that it made me want to pick up sticks and try it myself. Then I became a metalhead, and it was all about how quickly I could play! But it was the basic rhythm that initially drew me in. I don't think I've gone in that way again with my drumming since Nevermind, and I'm extremely pleased of being a simple drummer.' When Nevermind surpassed both Guns N' Roses' Use Your Illusions and U2's Achtung Baby to top the American album chart, it was clear that Nirvana had made an enduring effect on rock music as we know it in only a few short months. But there were issues going on behind the scenes. Nirvana, a British band from the 1960s, were upset that a new act had stolen' their name: another, Los Angeles-based band of the same name also stepped up and sought money to give their moniker: they received $50,000.

Like Cobain, Grohl had doubts about the band's huge popularity and the bandwagon-jumping followers already lampooned on 'In Bloom'. 'We didn't anticipate the album to do so well. We were quite aware that it went against the grain. I mean, the first thing that started frightening me off was going to shows and seeing redneck loggers in the front row. I had not anticipated such a large crowd.' More crucially, Dave developed a dread of flying, which, when combined with his newly acquired claustrophobia and 'conventional' stage fright, didn't improve his mood. His anxiety now was that hundreds of people would be inconvenienced by his incapacity to play, which was always a hurdle to clear before showtime. The triumph of 'Smells Like Teen Spirit' opened so many doors for Nirvana that it was unsurprising that the song was subjected to some in-depth scrutiny. But, from where he was, Dave couldn't agree with the reviewers' profound and important readings. Dave added to those tunes with some great stick-work - notably the cymbals at the conclusion of 'Come As You Are' and the snare-drum roll that marks the transition to the chorus in 'In Bloom'. Even Grohl's road manager, Alex Macleod, described him as "rock solid the whole time" and "a good influence" on his fellow band members. Barrett Jones was his drum tech at the time, so he had a friendly face to confide in when things went wrong.

The autumn/winter 1991 European tour to promote Nevermind left Nirvana with stress fractures that would never fully heal. Much of this was owing to Courtney Love's presence, who was touring Europe with Hole at the same time. She would even cancel gigs to spend time with Kurt, and the action was so severe that his roommate Dave was compelled to seek refuge with road manager Macleod, who was hardly his favorite person by all accounts. Every triumph comes with its own set of pressures, and thoughts are already going to the next record. 'I always envisioned our second record as being much less manufactured, where we could push the sound even farther and see if we could get a noisy LP into the charts,' Dave told Melody Maker in July 1992. But this was no problem for Kurt. Dave Grohl had achieved success at an age (23) when he was ready to accept it. He wasn't going to let the stress get to him. 'Our main job, in my opinion, is not to be someone we are not. Pretending to be a professional rock band does not seem to work for me. Let's have a bad show if we're going to have a shitty show. I understand tha being a part of a huge concert comes with a lot of responsibility, bu what about other kinds? I'm not sure. It becomes a burden once yot consider it an obligation.' These are wise words. However, event would now follow their own course.

CHAPTER 2
The Zeppelin Explodes

When it came to music, he was willing to provide 25%, which woulc be split between his rhythm section. This amounted to 6.75 percen each song - not a particularly large offer, but one he claimed wa: non-negotiable. One critic summed up Grohl and Novoselic': feelings as 'betrayed, bullied, and humiliated,' after learning that th arrangement would be backdated to include Nevermind. During the band's two-week summer tour of Europe in 1992, Gold Mountair management sent out minders' to ensure Kurt behaved himself. Kur and Courtney were more isolated as a result, and Kurt entered rehat not long after their return to the United States. Meanwhile Courtney's band Hole had been signed for a rumored million dollars which was more than Nirvana had received.

Dave considers the show to be his favorite Nirvana performance 'There were rumors that the band was breaking up, Kurt was ir treatment, and we were self-destructing. We went onstage in front o1 60,000 people without practicing and delivered one of our bes' performances yet. The year 1992 came to an end with the publicatior of Incesticide, a collection of B-sides, radio sessions, and odditie: that suited their record label's desire to release something for the Christmas market. The album includes recordings by all four o1 Nirvana's drummers, demonstrating not only the enormous rise ir clout when Grohl took over at the kit, but also how important he wa: to the band's success. Dave may be heard on 'Been a Son, 'Turnaround,' 'Molly's Lips,' 'Son of a Gun,' '(New Wave) Polly,' anc 'Aneurysm,' all of which were recorded for BBC Radio 1's John Pee in October 1990 (shortly after Dave's arrival) and Mark Goodier a1 the end of 1991. When Michael Azerrad interviewed Dave for Come As You Are: The Story of Nirvana, he was candid. It wa: commissioned in an attempt to recount the tale from the band's perspective, and it was initially released in October 1993, when Kurt was still alive, and it lived up to the anticipation of being 'by far the most intimate look ever at one of the most influential pop-music groups to emerge in years.' The drummer said that it was a waste of time for him to show up to interviews for the first year or so since Krist 'had a lot to say... Kurt had the beyond-clever bursts of wit... and I was like a paperweight.' He confessed that, even at this point, he didn't consider himself a vital member of the band.

Nirvana performed at San Francisco's Cow Palace in April 1993 to raise awareness and funds for rape survivors in Bosnia and Herzegovina. The bill also included L7, the Breeders, and Disposable Heroes of Hiphoprisy. However, this was not to be a year of huge live activity, with expectations for their as-yet-unwritten new album reaching comical proportions. The album, In Utero, was finally released on September 21st. Nevermind had sold nine million copies by early 1994, despite an initial pressing of only 40,000. Kurt was never going to make a carbon replica, and he made that clear by replacing producer Butch Vig with Steve Albini. Dave was the simplest Nirvana member to work with, according to Steve Albini. He praised his 'rock solid' drums, telling Michael Azerrad that seeing Grohl play drums was 'perhaps the highlight of my enthusiasm for the band.' Dave was also described as a 'nice, very silly guy to be around.'

Dave's playing benefited greatly from Albini's strategy of positioning a large number of mics about the room to maximize natural reverb, resulting in a sound far apart from the previous album's studio-enhanced shine. He revealed to Azerrad that the answer was a combination of 'a talented drummer... and a kit that sounds nice acoustically.' This was the straightforward yet effective strategy that ensured In Utero was acoustically light years ahead of its platinum predecessor. Dave was impressed by the fact that, whereas Nevermind songs featured a verse and chorus that were often repeated, the new album featured significantly more words, indicating that Cobain had a lot more to say. According to Grohl, the singer has gone from 'adolescent anguish to rock-star agony... Kurt believes he's backed up against a wall and he's just going to scream his way out.' The initial title of the album, 'I Hate Myself and Want to Die,' was changed, but the tone of the songs remained bleak.

The recording took place at Pachyderm Studios in Cannon Falls, Minnesota, and cost a total of $24,000. Albini accepted a $100,000 flat fee, despite the fact that a royalty would have paid him significantly more. On Valentine's Day 1993, recording sessions began, and basic recordings and overdubs were done in a week, after which Albini spent a few days mixing the songs. Kurt later described it as "the easiest recording [Nirvana] had ever done" in Azerrad's Come As You Are. Grohl, like his bandmates, praised the finished product's sonic quality. 'This album reminds me of Nirvana! Nevermind's main issue was that it didn't have any. When compared to the enormous boom, rumble, and khhhhhhh of our live tapes, it's a crisp, thin thing. 'Boom and rumble in utero, guy!'

At least four of the songs - 'Dumb,' 'Pennyroyal Tea,' 'Radio Friendly Unit Shifter,' and 'All Apologies' - were written three years prior, implying Kurt was struggling to come up with new material. Despite this, only one tune - 'Scentless Apprentice,' credited to Cobain/Grohl/Novoselic - had any other input, however a secret track named 'Gallons of Rubbing Alcohol Flow Through the Strip' was also a group composition. A jam recorded in Rio de Janeiro in January 1993, it was included on UK and Australian copies of In Utero and begins about 20 minutes after the finish of 'All Apologies'. Dave had contributed the main guitar riff to 'Scentless Apprentice,' and while Kurt admitted in a late 1993 MTV interview that the riff was initially 'kind of boneheaded,' he was pleased with how the song developed and hoped Novoselic and Grohl would contribute more to the band's songwriting in the future.

While the availability of a best-selling single in 'Teen Spirit' aided sales of Nevermind, no similar tune appeared on the follow-up long-player. Nonetheless, In Utero was the album of 1993, just as Nevermind was the album of 1992. (It was released in late 1991, but let's not be too technical.) Utero reached Number One in the United Kingdom (where it went gold) and the United States (where it went five times platinum), was ranked third in Rolling Stone's year-end album chart, and charted in Sweden, Australia, New Zealand, Portugal, Finland, Norway, Holland, and Austria. The 'Heart Shaped

Box' single, which reached Number Five in Britain, was remarkable in providing Dave his first solo Nirvana writing credit in the shape of a B-side titled 'Marigold'. Kurt had overheard him working on the tune, which was originally titled 'Color Pictures of a Marigold,' and thought it had promise. It was recorded during the sessions for In Utero after the two jammed on it. Grohl has reached a tiny but vital milestone. 'Three potential responses to this record: a) this is Nirvana's pretentious noise, we want to destroy our career record; b) this is brilliant, now we can see Nevermind was clearly not a true representation of this band; and c) we don't like Nirvana anyway, and this one sucks twice as bad!'

Dave had taken a break from the mayhem in the summer of 1993 to explore the world with his soon-to-be bride Jennifer Youngblood. They'd had time to vacation in Italy and rode motorcycles across America before Dave reunited with his former band Scream for a fortnight: "Humping our own gear into CBGB's and sleeping on friends' floors renewed my faith.' Nirvana began a three-month tour of North America on October 18, 1993. Kurt introduced new musicians, including a second guitarist from the Germs, Pat Smear, and strings. 'Having Pat on stage has freed me up to spend more time engaging with the audience,' Kurt remarked, quickly adding that he didn't see himself 'ever being Mick Jagger.' Dave was really excited about this new breakthrough. 'We had been looking for a second guitar player in Nirvana for a long time,' explains Grohl. 'We thought it would be fantastic if we could get Steve Turner from Mudhoney, Buzz [Osborne] from the Melvins, or Eugene [Kelly] from Eugenius. Grohl would later bring the newbie into the Foo Fighters lineup. Krist Novoselic, for the record, is a Pat Smear fan: 'He's got a lot of personality and spunk, and that rubs off on the band,' he stated. Another newcomer, cellist Mori Goldstone, described his boss as "sort of depressive," but "basically seemed optimistic and had ideas for the future." 'I think,' he said emphatically, 'he was rather overwhelmed in general by his fame.'

MTV Unplugged, taped on the nights of November 18 and 19, 1993 at Sony Studios in New York for transmission by the cable television behemoth, would provide a lasting reminder of this tour. Established performers such as Eric Clapton, Rod Stewart, and Neil Young found career-revitalizing success by appearing on 'Unplugged' recordings and releasing the results on compact disc. The performance, which aired on December 16, 1993, had Nirvana performing songs from several albums, including one from Bleach, four from Nevermind, and three from In Utero. The remaining six songs were cover versions, including three by legendary Phoenix punk band the Meat Puppets, as well as one each by David Bowie ('The Man Who Sold the World,' the Vaselines, and blues artist Leadbelly ('Where Did You Sleep Last Night?,' a tune Kurt had played in Aberdeen). 'Dumb' and 'Polly' had strings attached, whilst the gloomy, moving 'Pennyroyal Tea' was sung by Cobain alone. The studio version was supposed to be Nirvana's next single from In Utero, but it never came out. This performance rekindled that lost luster and restored it to its due place in the spotlight.

The show's audio was published as Unplugged in New York in October 1994, months after Kurt Cobain's death, and quickly rose to the top of the charts. It's impossible to determine how it would have been received if it had been published under different conditions. Kurt certainly seemed to be 'cleaning his palate' before beginning on some new course - with or without Nirvana, it was impossible to determine. In January 1994, Nirvana gathered at Bob Lang Studios in North Seattle for what would turn out to be their final recording session. Unfortunately, Dave and Krist had to spend two of the three days waiting for Kurt to arrive. This irritated Dave, but also provided him the opportunity to record some of his own music, most notably 'Exhausted' and 'Big Me'. Kurt arrived on the third day, and numerous new songs were attempted. One of them, 'You Know You're Right,' was finished to the point that it could be featured on the 'Nirvana' compilation album, which was released eight years later. However, this was the final cut. Nirvana, the out-of-control train, was ready to crash the buffers.

PART 4
Cruising

CHAPTER 1
Crossing the Bridge to Washington

HOW IN THE WORLD DID I GET HERE?
The Kennedy Center Honors have been regarded as America's most prominent performing arts awards presentation since 1978, honoring artists in music, dance, theater, opera, film pictures, and television for their lifetime achievements to American culture. To be involved in any capacity is an honor in and of itself. Most award ceremonies I attend make me feel like I'm crashing the party, with security escorting me out to the parking lot after one drink. But, no matter how out of my element I am, I have never been afraid to strike up a conversation with the most unexpected people. All performers are required to be shuttled to and from the Kennedy Center on one of those large buses that tourists usually fill to visit Washington's most popular attractions, except instead of gangs of blue-haired seniors from the Midwest, the bus is filled with America's most recognizable artists, usually breaking into a roaring version of "99 Bottles of Beer on the Wall" (take it from me, the song truly acquires a whole new life when sung by Sting). It's seldom a lengthy journey to the gig, but it's always just long enough to get to know these familiar faces and become good friends, swapping stories of illustrious careers and getting hearing aid advice from the best of them (thank you, Herbie).

As I strolled through the corridors behind the stage, I attempted to visualize all of the voices that had filled these sacred chambers since their inception in 1971, asking myself, "How on earth did I get here?" Not previous DC punk rock gangsters, but America's most prestigious performers, were housed in this building. I didn't agree with all of the ideas and values that some of these individuals spent their days debating, so I followed my mother's advice and avoided the three things that we were always instructed not to discuss at any dinner table: money, politics, and religion. This was a weekend when everyone could see each other as more than a Democrat or a Republican. We were all, first and foremost, human beings, and nothing brings people together like music and art.

FUCK, I SAID. MADELEINE ALBRIGHT WILL THINK I'M A DUMMY.

As I passed through the receiving line, I was already dreading my time at the platform as I shook hands with current Secretary of State Condoleezza Rice, another thing I never imagined happening in my wildest dreams. My deep childhood fear about being thought of a foolish kicked in as I looked around the room full of scholars and intellectual titans, and I began to second-guess myself. I held that awful speech in my hands like a string of prayer beads as I sat at my table with other senators and cabinet officials, calculating the minutes till my most gruesome public execution. I sat and watched a each speaker, one by one, delivered a long, beautiful discourse worthy of any inaugural or State of the Union speech... knowing that I would soon be the only jackass in the room to use the word "dude." With barely a few minutes to spare, I came up with an idea: The Who's distinctive reversal of musical roles was what set them apart from other bands. Keith Moon's lyrical drumming resembled the vocalist, Pete Townshend's solid rhythm guitar resembled the drummer, John Entwistle's unconventional bass soloing resembled the lead guitarist, and Roger Daltrey's muscular vocals unified the band like a conductor for a fire orchestra. This could work, I reasoned. I must admit, I was no Bob Schieffer that night, but I did manage to avoid any rotten tomatoes and a solitary "dude," and may have even received a smile from Madeleine Albright.

I FELT LIKE I WAS SEEING HISTORY, SO I ASKED MYSELF AGAIN, HOW ON EARTH DID I GET HERE?

The last thing left to do before traveling to the gig was to pose for a photo with the president and First Lady in front of the White House Christmas tree. This was a decision that required more than a second of thought. To put it gently, my personal politics do not fit with those of the present government, therefore I was uncomfortable about participating in a photo with the president. In 2010, President Barack Obama presented Paul McCartney with the Library of Congress Gershwin Prize, which is given to just one person each year for their lifetime contribution to popular music. It's the American equivalent of being knighted, and it's possibly the highest accolade for musicians. There was a performance planned in the East Room of the White House (I guess I was becoming a regular), and I was invited to come sing "Band on the Run" with Paul on a tiny stage in that small room full of people. Of course, I leaped at the chance to jam with Paul, not only because he is the reason I became a musician, but also because he's a lot of fun to jam with.

When I arrived at Lisner Auditorium for rehearsals (just across the street from Tower Records, where I used to work part-time), I was met onstage by his gorgeous band and crew, and after some catching up, the musical director approached to introduce himself. I was reasonably prepared, but I believed Paul and his band would do all the heavy lifting anyhow, so if I forgot a line or chord, I probably wouldn't even be in the PA.

YOU FAKE IT TILL YOU MAKE IT AGAIN.
We went through a few versions until it was "good enough for grunge" (a ridiculous phrase that's been floating around the Foo Fighters for years), and then I went back to my hotel room to practice the song on repeat until I felt comfortable playing it to the two most important people on the planet, who would be sitting shoulder to shoulder six feet in front of me. This was a huge one, and it wasn't some ramshackle side-stage lineup. Stevie Wonder, Elvis Costello, Jack White, Emmylou Harris, and Faith Hill were all performing Paul's songs for the occasion, and I was overwhelmed by the caliber of talent on show. It was without a doubt the most nerve-racking experience I'd ever experienced, and for good cause. The musicians milled around the White House during soundcheck the morning of the event, cheering each other on and marveling at the size of the miniscule stage, which was only two feet high and just big enough to fit Paul's band. When it was over, I was free to go around the White House, enjoying the historic pictures and perusing the books in the little library downstairs. On the night of the performance, all of the performers waited in an adjoining room for their time to play, much like a line of paratroopers waiting to leap out of an airplane and into the sky. They were introduced one by one as they walked through the closely packed crowd to that tiny little stage where they would

greet Paul and the president before performing their song. I couldn't be the only one who was nervous here, I reasoned. I felt almost naked without the Foo Fighters' wall of sound behind me.

I DID NOT WISH TO WASTE THIS MOMENT. I resolved to quit wondering, "How did I get here?" I was present. I told myself I wasn't going to waste any time being terrified or wishing I was somewhere else. The long journey from my childhood in Springfield, Virginia, to cutting my teeth as a musician in the Washington, DC, music scene, to performing in the White House for a Beetle and a president made this the most full-circle moment of my life, but instead of getting lost in complicated introspection, I simply smiled. My name was called, and I felt a sense of serenity wash over me. I stepped to the platform with my head held high and stood proudly in front of Paul and the president, feeling like the happiest person on the planet to have been here, past and present, right and left, bridged together in song.

CHAPTER 2
Down Under DUI

It was January 2000, and the Foo Fighters were in Australia for the Big Day Out, Australia's largest annual tour, which began in 1992 with a Sydney-only show featuring Nirvana and the Violent Femmes, and eventually grew to a massive three-week, six-city extravaganza hosting up to a hundred bands each year. It was the top of any touring band's itinerary, set in the blistering heat of the magnificent Aussie summer, given the casual pace of six gigs in three weeks, making it more of a vacation in the sun than the typical hard tempo we were all used to. We dubbed it "The Big Day Off," and we made the most of every opportunity offstage. My fiancée had traveled down from the United States for a quick vacation, and she had her heart set on seeing a well-known French psychic who resided in an apartment complex outside of Sydney. She had apparently visited her before on another tour to Australia with her own band years ago, and this person was the real deal, according to those familiar with the phenomenon. Over the years, our old friend/promoter Stephen Pavlovic had brought other mystical musicians to her, all of whom had returned home with wonderful assessments of her perceptive abilities.

When we returned, my girlfriend was fatigued from her reading, and the psychic swiftly switched her attention to me, as I had obviously been a difficult topic of conversation while we were away. Because she spoke very little English and required translation, my girlfriend and I had an unpleasant relationship as I relied on her (a Montreal local) to explain the psychic's most private disclosures, no matter how uncomfortable they were for her to hear. My hands, according to my new clairvoyant best buddy, shone with a bright blue aura. Whether I believed her or not, I was ecstatic, if not pleased, by her telepathic declaration. How could I have missed this? I pondered. I could have used my powerful blue aura all along! Then she raised her head and inquired if I had seen any ghosts.

This was a challenging question to answer. Had I ever been visited by a traditional floating apparition who had crossed over from the other side to retake its former land in a cliché haunting? No. Had I been witness to a series of unexplained incidents in which I thought I was in the presence of something neither alive nor dead? Yes. It was situated among dense pines at the end of a dead-end street, just blocks from the magnificent Puget Sound, a pretty modest and unassuming house at first appearance. However, upon entering, you were greeted by an architectural masterpiece. Multiple levels of landings and rooms framed in beautiful wood, all flooded with natural light from skylights placed into the great ceilings and massive windows overlooking the dense forest outside. The first night at the house, I sat on my old futon with my back against the bedroom wall, viewing my new television (real rock & roll excess!). The rain was falling in sheets, and I was getting a little anxious about being alone in this vast mansion, when the house rocked with a huge BANG! It wasn't lightning or thunder, nor was it an explosion from outside. I had goosebumps all over my body from terror as I tiptoed silently from one room to the next, expecting to find proof of a break-in, but there was none. When I got back to bed, I turned off the TV and slept with one eye open for the rest of the night. I had never felt this way before and told myself that it was just my wild imagination—that is, until I discovered that I was not the only one who had experienced this common and terrifying incident.

I eventually settled in and proceeded to fill the house with modest furnishings, enough to host a Halloween dinner party at my new dining room table. We agreed to relate ghost stories over cocktails after dinner, some personal, some not, but I kept my thoughts about this brand-new house to myself. As much as I was relieved to hear that I wasn't the only one who had this sensation, that maybe I wasn't insane after all, I took it as confirmation that this wonderful first home I'd purchased was fucking haunted. I wasn't planning on leaving anytime soon, and while I didn't mind sharing a house with my old friend Barrett, sharing a house with a ghost was not something I had signed up for. Then the dreams started. It was always the same woman, dressed in a faded gray sweater and a dark blue wool skirt. Her dark, wiry hair was twisted and disheveled, and she stood there barefoot, never uttering a word, staring at me with her piercing eyes and a deep grief.

But I stayed for years and became accustomed to the sound of footsteps on the wooden kitchen floor, motion detectors going off for no apparent reason, and the rare door opening by itself. Friends sent me heaps of sage to rid the house of evil spirits, but it went untouched since I wasn't going down that rabbit hole, and it smelled like cat piss. To keep things easy, I informed the psychic that I did not always "see" spirits. She then inquired as to whether I had seen any UFOs. This was certainly something I was interested in. After all, I named my band the Foo Fighters after the World War II slang term for unidentified flying objects; our record label imprint is called Roswell Records after the 1947 UFO crash in Roswell, New Mexico; and my publishing company is called MJ Twelve Music, which is a reference to Harry S. Truman's alleged secret committee of scientists, military leaders, and government officials assembled to recover and investigate alien spacecraft. So I was well-versed in the world of UFO conspiracies, despite the fact that I had never seen one myself.

I ASKED MY FRIEND FOR TRANSLATION, AND SHE SAID, "THOSE ARE NOT DREAMS."
I immediately remembered the innumerable intense dreams I'd had as a child about being visited by extraterrestrials, which I can still remember vividly to this day. I used to imagine myself soaring through my neighborhood, peering down at the rows of tiny dwellings below from the window of a small craft, silently hovering and blasting through the air at incredible speeds with ease, invisible to the human sight. But there is one dream that I will never forget, a dream so powerful and deeply involved that I can't get it out of my head. It was a lovely early evening in a southern European beach town, and the sky was a wonderful shade of cerulean blue in the twilight hour between sunset and full night. The stars were just visible, brightening with each passing instant as the sun set behind the water, when the sky burst in a blinding light, sending me to the ground. I looked up and saw thousands of UFOs darting across the sky, all different sizes, shapes, and colors, and I sat there in awe, taking in this incredible event while looking around at the incredulous faces of thousands of others doing the same thing. Time had stopped.

Through some type of telepathy, a thunderous voice thundered into my head. "THE EVOLUTION OF MAN," the voice said as animated graphics were projected into the sky, explaining how beings from a faraway corner of the universe aided our species' evolution. On the left side of the sky, Leonardo da Vinci's drawing Vitruvian Man was projected, and on the right, a map of the world with all of our borders and territories redrawn, while a voice announced this event to be the "DAWN OF A NEW ERA." I was moved, but the most traction this dream ever had in my life was as the basis for the Foo Fighters' video for "The Sky Is a Neighborhood," which I directed and stars my two children Violet and Harper. It was a great dream, I thought, but it was only a dream. Until now, that is. According to the psychic, this was not my imagination, but rather reality. We concluded my session, said our goodbyes, and drove back to Sydney from her modest flat. These revelations gave me confidence, and I wondered if this was something I was born with, thinking of all the times I could have used my psychic gift to help me. Including the previous week on the Gold Coast.

The Gold Coast, a Queensland seaside town 45 minutes south of Brisbane, is Australia's equivalent to Fort Lauderdale, Florida. Beach bars brimming with blazing, neon-colored beverages, blond-haired surfers wearing half-off wetsuits at every turn, and, yes, a Sea World theme park for the more family-oriented guests. We milked every second in this bronzed utopia for every last drop of mischief we could find, and because we were down to play the Big Day Off tour we had plenty of time to take advantage of its juvenile trappings. Taylor and I opted to hire scooters upon arrival so that we could whizz around town throughout the day, beach to beach, for the three days leading up to our major gig at the Gold Coast Parklands, a greyhound racing track only a few miles from the city.

As we were preparing for the gig, I had another insane idea: I was going to drive my scooter onstage during our performance and rev the engine like Rob Halford from Judas Priest had always done, but with a massive Harley-Davidson motorcycle, to pay tribute to the heavy metal king himself. I went back to the dressing room after the show and looked at the schedule of artists that was tacked to the wall. I spotted one of my favorite bands, the Hellacopters from Sweden, were performing on a side stage in the distance, so I grabbed a couple beers, placed Bobby Gillespie from Primal Scream on the back of my now-famous scooter, and we putted over to see them play. The Hellacopters, a hard rock bombardment of classic riffs and classic hair, never failed to put on a terrific show, and I was fortunate enough to see many of them having toured extensively with them over the years.

All those years of getting away with the most jackass shit you could imagine and never getting caught, and here I was in Australia being arrested for drunk driving on a fucking moped. "Pull over and take it out of gear!" he instructed. I couldn't help but laugh. Gears? There were no gears on this thing. To get the blasted thing moving, you had to use your feet like Fred Flintstone. I set it on its kickstand, and the police requested my identification. This was now a problem. I never, ever travel with my passport because I would lose it in a hot New York minute.

MAYBE FOR ONE TIME, THIS ROCK STAR NAME-DROP WOULD WORK. NOPE.
"Musician, huh?" he asked, with a newfound confidence. I explained that we were on the Big Day Out tour and had been in his lovely city for a few days, hence the ludicrous scooter. "Ah...," he admitted. "When's the next show?" "Tomorrow in Sydney," I said, a spark of hope in my eyes. "Sorry, mate, but you're going to miss that one." I'm going to have to take you to jail." Panic ensued. I said that from where we were standing, I could practically see the hotel and that I could easily park this piece of trash and walk the rest of the way. "Sorry, mate," was all I received back. I had been fucked.

I was shortly handcuffed, placed in the back of a police car, and brought across the street to a mobile police station, where I was interrogated by investigators as if I were Ted Bundy. "Can you tell me your home address?" What is the address of your mother's house? "Can you tell me where your mother works?" It went on for a long time, and if I did have a buzz, it was soon wearing off due to the monotonous and completely useless questioning. After what seemed like hours, I thought, "Just throw me in the goddamned cell." When I got to the jail, all of the other criminals from the show cheered me on as I was properly booked at the front desk and thrown in a cell with a passed-out punter in a Primus T-shirt who snored so loudly that I felt I might have to hang myself with my shoelaces. Shivering from the chilly wet clothes I had been wearing all night in the rain, I retired to my concrete slab of a bed and did my best to put the stiff complementary canvas blanket they had given me around my body. But my criminal career was far from over. I was obligated by law to return to the Gold Coast a week later for my court date. If convicted, I would not only have to pay a fine, but I could also face jail time, not to mention jeopardize my chances of ever being able to visit their lovely nation again, which was the most terrible thought because Australia had become my favorite place to vacation over the years.

I would never be able to forgive myself or my band if I blew that opportunity because of a few beers and a cheap scooter. I began to take this all very seriously, so seriously that Gus and I went to a department store and spent $700 on a suit so I wouldn't look like a complete jerk in front of the cops. We met my lawyer, or "barrister," as they are known in the legal world, at a Burger King near the courthouse and discussed my defense over greasy cheeseburgers and stale fries. There wasn't much else to say. I went over the speed limit in a car. The case is closed. There were no questionable technicalities on which I could rely to dismiss my case, so it was essentially up to the court to determine the harshness of my sentence (and the wisdom of my suit selection). We went over to the gallows for judgment day, and I straightened my cheap tie. This was becoming serious. The book was thrown at me by the judge. I luckily avoided jail time or community service, but technically there was a conviction, so I paid my fine (less than the suit!) and am now eternally labeled a criminal in Australia, which means that anytime I visit their country, I have to tick the small box that reads, "I am a criminal."

I THOUGHT I GOT OFF EASY. MY ACTUAL SENTENCE? LIFE IS RIDICULOUS.
If I had used my clairvoyant talent that night on the rainy highway, freezing in my hoodie as I approached the sobriety checkpoint, I wouldn't have had to answer for this shameful crime for years to come. Mine is a small cost to pay... But, ever since that meeting with the psychic in Sydney, I've wondered if the tremendous blue aura

that appears to radiate from my calloused hands will ever aid me. Despite my alleged superpowers, I will always opt to let life run its natural course, a journey with no road map to refer to if you get lost.

CHAPTER 3
Life was accelerating.

I'd only lately recognized my addiction, admitting that maybe five pots of coffee a day was a little excessive, but I hadn't embraced the catastrophic repercussions until now. Regrettably, I am THAT man. Give me one, and I'll take 10. There's a reason I've never done cocaine, because I know deep down that if I used coke the way I drink coffee, I'd be sucking dicks at the bus stop every morning for an eight ball. But it wasn't only the coffee that sent me to the hospital on that particular day. Life was accelerating. 2009 was a fantastic year. It all started with my 40th birthday party, which was held at the Medieval Times theme restaurant in Anaheim, California, a massive equestrian arena where you can watch fake knights with fake English accents joust while eating greasy turkey legs with your bare hands and drinking Coors Light from BeDazzled chalices. It is the most absurd, hilarious, and downright embarrassing dining experience known to man, and apparently not somewhere a grown man would typically celebrate another trip around the sun, which I didn't realize until the fake king's voice came booming over the PA with a few announcements. "Ladies and gentlemen, tonight we have a few birthdays!" Eddie is seven years old! Tommy is ten years old! And Dave is about to turn... forty?"

I met Josh in the early 1990s while he was playing guitar in one of my favorite bands of all time, Kyuss, and we had since toured the world together with his band Queens of the Stone Age, which I had even joined for a short time, recording their album Songs for the Deaf and playing some of the most explosive shows of my entire life. Josh has "the thing," an indefinable, unspoken, magical ability that is truly one in a million, and whenever we played together, the result was always like a hypnotic wave of starlings, the music effortlessly flowing from one direction to the next, never losing its tight pattern. Our onstage improvisation was like two old friends finishing each other's sentences, frequently laughing uncontrollably behind each other's back at our musical inside jokes. In essence, it was a match made in heaven, and we would seize any opportunity to join forces.

Josh was also a drummer, so we could simply switch instruments while attempting to move as far away from the sound of Queens and the Foos as possible. But we knew we'd have a good time, and after a year and a half on the road playing "Learn to Fly" every single night, the promise of something exciting was much needed to keep me from abandoning music and being the terrible roofer I was destined to be. Around the same time, I was asked to present the members of Led Zeppelin with a GQ Outstanding Achievement Award (let the painfully obvious sentiment of that colossal understatement sink in for a moment), so I called Josh and asked if I should mention the idea of our secret project to John Paul Jones, the greatest, grooviest bassist in rock and roll history. Lo and behold, John decided to make the trip out to Los Angeles to see if we had the chemistry that I had imagined we would have, and his arrival coincided with my fantastically juvenile birthday party, so I invited him along for a medieval feast of greasy fast-food delights. If he can make it through this night of lowbrow theater and youthful antics without crashing at LAX, we might have a chance at something amazing. Bless his heart, he patiently tolerated my immaturity, and we met a few days later at Josh's studio, Pink Duck, for our first jam.

Harper Willow Grohl arrived in the world on April 17, 2009. From the start, she was a screaming ball of joy, so wonderful, so gorgeous. My understanding of love grew tenfold with her arrival, and I was once again a proud parent. I'd always loved life, but my new daughter made me love it even more, waking up enthusiastically every morning to see her gorgeous face, no matter how sleep deprived I was. I was happy to now have two beautiful girls and would jump at any chance to spend time with them, day or night, no matter how weary I was from my insane schedule of rushing from one studio to the next all day, drinking coffee like it was an Olympic event.

LIFE WAS SPEEDING UP.
As if all of this wasn't enough to send me to my death (HERE LIES DAVID ERIC GROHL. HE SHOULD HAVE SWITCHED TO SANKA), the Foo Fighters were invited to perform at the White House for a July 4 BBQ hosted by freshly elected President Obama for our military families. It was an opportunity I couldn't pass up, set

on the groomed South Lawn overlooking the monuments of th National Mall, for a variety of personal reasons. After all, this wa my hometown, and I'd spent countless Fourth of Julys on the othe side of that White House fence, watching the magnificent firework display above from a blanket in the grass while the Beach Boy played on a festival stage in the distance, or attending punk roc concerts at the base of the Lincoln Memorial as an angry teenage exercising my right to protest on the day when it might have mean the most. But this was unique. In addition, I was refurbishing m home. With my ever-expanding family, my once-large house bega to seem cramped. So plans were established to transform previousl insignificant rooms into something more kid-friendly (and... ahem. a studio for myself where we would one day record our albun *Wasting Light*). Violet was three years old at the time, and Harpe was just three months old, so considerable rearrangement wa required to accommodate them, which necessitated some majo work. Construction is quite loud.

LIFE WAS SPEEDING UP.
My new schedule went something like this for weeks: A baby and three-year-old demanding my complete attention at the crack o dawn, while buzz saws and jackhammers thunder in the distance Make yourself a cup of coffee. Drink the coffee and dash straight t the Foo Fighters' studio. Make yourself another cup of coffee. Begi working. Arrive in the Vultures' studio, throw on another pot, an consume that for the next four hours while I bash the living shit ou of my drums in an attempt to impress John Paul Jones. Drive home trembling like a leaf from the four thousand milligrams of caffein I've just taken over the course of eighteen hours, and tr unsuccessfully to get at least four hours of sleep before waking u and repeating the process. And so forth, ad nauseam, on loop.

LIFE WAS SPEEDING UP.
This unpleasant moment of my developing dilemma is bes appreciated by seeing the now-infamous YouTube clip "Fresh Pots, a two-minute short film put together by our old friend and comrad Liam Lynch, who was present during the Vultures record' production. I recall the first ache. I was in my hallway at home fretting about the deafening remodeling that shook the house lik

dropping bombs, when it hit me like a knife in my rib cage. I came to a halt and lifted my palm to my chest, scared that I was suffering a heart attack but hoping it was simply a torn muscle from all of the drumming I'd been doing with the Vultures. (I now know better than to self-diagnose using a random blogger's homemade website.) I didn't have ALL of the symptoms, but I was clearly feeling something serious, so I looked up heart attack prevention methods and chose to keep it a secret. After all, I wasn't going to miss this White House gig for anything. Even a heart attack couldn't keep me from flying home and performing for the president. I slipped two aspirin in my wallet and didn't say anything.

LIFE WAS SPEEDING UP.
When I arrived at the White House, the lovely heat of DC's oppressive summer air almost healed the anguish in my chest, and as we prepared to soundcheck on the lawn, I looked out over the fence to the monuments I had once taken for granted. The Washington Monument, looming in the distance like a maypole around which the city performs its intricate dance. In the annual rebirth of spring, the Jefferson Memorial is graced by rows of cherry blossoms. And the Lincoln Memorial, where I went to numerous Fourth of July performances as a teenage punk rocker. These were not the Beach Boys; they were protest songs. The "Rock Against Reagan" concert, performed every Fourth of July during his presidency, was a gathering of punks from all over who came to sing along with their favorite bands in unison in opposition to the president's ultraconservative policies.

LIFE WAS SPEEDING UP.
We were escorted up to the house for the first time to meet Barack Obama, and as we walked into the Blue Room, overlooking the grill below, we were welcomed by the president and First Lady with a really down-to-earth, friendly, and kind greeting. Our visit to the White House had taken on new significance. That night, as we watched the fireworks from the balcony, I was overcome with emotion when I gazed up at the First Family standing on the balcony. History was being written. And as I saw my wife, children, and mother's lighted faces staring up into the sky, I was thrilled with pride, pleased to share this historic moment with them. And I was

flooded with affection for Pat, my most trusted and loyal buddy. We'd all gotten over the fence together.

LIFE WAS SPEEDING UP.

When I got back to Los Angeles, I called my doctor right away. "Dude, I've been having some chest pains," I explained. "Are you having them right now??" he asked, sounding more concerned than usual (and that's a lot). "Ummm... kinda...," I responded. He urged me to get in the car and drive to his office right away, so I sped out the door like Moses. After meeting with the doctor at Cedars and determining that there was no genuine threat, he advised me to take it easy. Even though I felt invincible, I was no superman, and I needed to take care of myself in order to take care of those I cared about. My love of life could be a little too much at times, pushing myself a little too far, but if I wanted to stay around for a while, I needed to be more aware of my mortal boundaries. What is his prescription? "Play the drums only three times per week, have a glass of wine before bed, and avoid coffee."

TWO OUT OF THREE IS NOT A BAD RATIO. DECAF IS AMAZING.

And life is still accelerating.

CHAPTER 4
Swing Dancing with AC/DC

"Do you mind if AC/DC comes to dinner?" This text from my wife, Jordyn, will go down in history as the most bizarre, absurd, and painfully apparent question I have ever been asked. AC/DC during dinner? The band that almost never appears in public, only to materialize on gigantic stages equipped with massive exploding cannons and massive amplifiers packed to the rafters? I should be aware. I was among them. Let There Be Rock was released in 1980 in an unknowing world of overly glamorized pop music, and it immediately made its way to all of the hip movie houses across the country that screened midnight movies on weekends. (A long-forgotten phenomena that most of my generation remembers as a stoner rite of passage. Some of my favorites were The Rocky Horror Picture Show, The Wall, and Heavy Metal.) The film is a tour de force, with the world's grittiest, grooviest no-bullshit hard rock band offering up a megadose of sweat, denim, and high-voltage rock and roll. It was filmed in Paris only a few months before the death of their original lead vocalist, Bon Scott. If you wanted to learn how to kick fucking ass and take fucking names, this was the master class for you.

I was already familiar with AC/DC at eleven years old, since their albums Dirty Deeds Done Dirt Cheap and Highway to Hell were two of my most treasured CDs in my increasing collection, so this movie was something I had to see. The Washington Post reported that the video was screened as part of the Wall of Sound concert series at the historic Uptown Theater in Washington, DC. So Larry Hinkle, my best buddy at the time, and I made a night of it, chauffeured downtown by his father in their burgundy Datsun 280ZX, the poor man's Porsche. Knowing it was the Wall of Sound concert series, we were tempted to sit near the sound system up front, but we chose a seat further back so we wouldn't have to strain our slender necks to see the enormous screen. Thank goodness, since we had no idea there was a concert-sized PA hiding behind those curtains, and as the house lights went down, it became clear that this was no ordinary matinée showing of Star Wars. After the last note of a concert has been played and the audience has gone home to the comfort of their warm beds, it's these brave souls who go to work coiling miles of cables and packing tons of equipment into battered road cases while wading through your littered beer cups and cigarette butts before passing out in bunks the size of coffins, getting just enough sleep to set it all back up the next morning.

I had never gone to a rock concert before, so I had no idea the strength of that level of noise could shake your rib cage with earthquake intensity. Needless to say, it appealed to me. A lot. My ears were already ringing by the time the band took the stage with their first song, "Live Wire," and I was on the edge of my seat.
I WANTED TO RIP THAT THEATER TO SHREDS. The adrenaline coursing through my veins triggered what can only be described as the change that Bruce Banner would go through when transforming into the Hulk in the late 1970s TV series. I couldn't stop myself from feeling overwhelmed and empowered by the sheer intensity of the music. I would have ripped the seat out of the floor and smashed it in the aisle if my skinny little arms had the strength, but instead I sat there shivering in my sneakers as AC/DC did what they do best: give every ounce of themselves to the audience and leave nothing behind.

This was incredible, I thought. Forget about the bands who merely stood there and fiddled with their instruments like medieval minstrels; these guys assaulted them as if it were their final day on Earth. I was a different boy by the time the credits rolled. I THOUGHT IF I'M GOING TO PLAY MUSIC IN A BAND, I'M GOING TO DO IT LIKE THAT. AC/DC happened to be in town in 2015 to perform their new song "Rock or Bust" at the 57th Annual Grammy Awards. I wasn't performing that night; instead, I was presenting an award, but as a lifelong AC/DC fan, I was far more anxious to see them than any of the other pretty monotonous pop acts with their absurd, Vegas-style displays. The show needed a big dose of good old-fashioned rock and roll. I'd be there, front and center, feeling the same overwhelming rush of adrenaline that had made me want to rip the Uptown Theater to shreds 35 years before (except now I'd be shoulder to shoulder with Katy Perry and Tony Bennett, feeling like I was hiding my flickering lighter at the end of a homemade pipe).

I NEVER GO A DAY WITHOUT THANKING THE UNIVERSE FOR THESE OTHERWORLDLY BLESSINGS, AND I MAKE IT A POINT TO TAKE NOTHING FOR GRANTED. Being a part of such a waking dream will never feel "normal" to me; it will always feel like I'm witnessing life from above, looking down at someone else's fantasy unfolding before me. But it is mine, and it is at these moments that I strive to be present, reminding myself that I am possibly the luckiest person on the planet to be able to take the next breath that will bring me to the next adventure. I received another text a few days before the show from my dear buddy Ben Jaffe of New Orleans' famed Preservation Hall Jazz Band, informing me that he was also in town for the Grammys and looking for a party. Nobody parties like a true New Orleans native, and nothing says New Orleans more than the Preservation Hall Jazz Band. Ben's father, Allan, founded them in the early 1960s, and they have epitomized the music, energy, and joy of their great city, keeping traditional New Orleans jazz alive for almost sixty years, playing three performances a night, three hundred sixty-five days a year. So, even when they put down their instruments (which they rarely do), the party never stops. In 2014, Foo Fighters had the distinction of spending a week recording their documentary series Sonic Highways in Preservation Hall, a pub that dates back to 1803. We all quickly became fast friends. By the end of that week, I had come to the conclusion that New Orleans is an American gem, and that we must all work together to preserve its unique culture steeped in European, Caribbean, and Cajun past. There is no place on Earth that has the absolute magic that New Orleans does. Without a question, it is my favorite city in the world.

The Preservation Hall Jazz Band had seven players, which indicated that at least 10 more people were needed. Of course, I would have loved to have them all, but we were on our way to taking over the entire fucking restaurant, so I responded with a timid "Uh, let me check," fearful that the restaurant would refuse our request for another 10 chairs. "How about we all come marching down the street playing in a second line, into the restaurant, straight to the table, and perform a set for you right there?" Ben said. There was no way t turn down such a great offer. A second-line parade is a distinctiv New Orleans art form, a practice dating back to the nineteent century in which a brass band marches down the street behind funeral procession to celebrate the life of a lost loved one. Today more informal versions of these parades may be found at any time o the streets of New Orleans, and if you hear the sound of syncopate funked-up jazz-swing approaching, grab a drink and join in. Yo never know where it will take you.

A sense of belonging and love, shared with people from all walks o life, united in rhythm and delight as we followed the music whereve it took us. On my first day in New Orleans, I was dancing down th street with strangers, smiling and bouncing to the music, when noticed a familiar face, Ben Jaffe, standing on top of a car in th distance. Jordyn and I dashed over to the restaurant after th Grammys to beat the crowd before our spectacular evening begar Our secret was mainly safe, but Paul was aware of it because, wel he is the all-knowing, all-seeing, omniscient, and almighty Pau McCartney. It turns out Paul had a relationship with Preservatio Hall dating back to his time in Wings, when he recorded at local ico Allen Toussaint's studio and would stop over to hang. "He was a so of regular for a while," Ben explained. I kept my phone nearby t coordinate the time of the band's entrance, ensuring sure everythin; was ready for the big reveal. The room began to fill up with th familiar faces of the individuals I care about the most. My mum, m pals, Paul... and then they appeared... AC/DC in person.

To be honest, I had previously met singer Brian Johnson, albei briefly, at a hotel bar in Valencia, Spain, on a day off from our Fo Fighters tour in 1996. We flowed out of the bus after a long drive o a day off and observed a few denim-clad autograph seekers standin; out front with stacks of photos and magazines to be signed. Standar procedure for any traveling band, but when we approached, w realized that they were completely engulfed in AC/DC paraphernali; and had no idea who we were. "You must adore AC/DC!" I chuckle; as we passed, and they revealed in their thick Spanish accents tha AC/DC was staying in our hotel since they were performing at th nearby Plaza de Toros de las Ventas bullfighting stadium that night which happened to be a rare night off for us. As we sipped our drinks at the hotel bar, a man in black pants, a black T-shirt, and a flat cap stepped into the beautiful room and ordered himself a drink while sitting alone on a barstool. We fell silent, stunned, for this was none other than THE Brian Johnson, the man who sang "Have a Drink on Me" from AC/DC's most cherished album, Back in Black.

That night, I finally got to see the AC/DC I fell in love with as an eleven-year-old dorky rock-and-roll worshiper. The amount of enthusiasm they demonstrated onstage was precisely what I had imagined, with Angus Young sprinting from one end of the massive stage decked with pyrotechnics and exploding cannons. The packed house only added to the spectacle, singing not just every line but also the guitar sections as they bounced like a rolling human wave to the rhythm of each song. It was awe-inspiring. Seeing all of these extremely prominent faces stream into our ramshackle after-Grammys party would have been enough to make me die happy, but knowing what was to come made it even sweeter. There was no way I could repay this room full of icons for the years of inspiration they had provided me, but if I could make them smile, dance, and feel the joy of music, like they had done for me my entire life, I would have made a little dent in my debt. The night continued until the early hours, and no matter how much we thought it would never end, the house lights came on, and it was time to return to reality, which seemed so far away after such a magnificent evening. I WAS EXHAUSTED—NOT PHYSICALLY, BUT MY SOUL HAD JUST FINISHED A TRIATHLON OF EMOTION, NOSTALGIA, AND ENDLESS LOVE FOR MUSIC. It's difficult to put into words my faith in music. It is good for me. A supernatural mystery in whose strength I will always have complete faith. And it is times like this that strengthen my faith. Don't only listen when you hear the procession coming down the street, spreading pleasure and love with every note; engage in the march. You never know where it will take you.

CHAPTER 5
Once again, I am inspired.

I am a firm believer in music's shared humanity, which I find more fulfilling than any other component of my work. When a one-dimensional image transforms into a living, breathing, three-dimensional human being, it fills your soul with hope that even our most beloved heroes are made of flesh and bone. I believe that people inspire others. That is why, when my admirers approach me, I feel the desire to connect with them. I, too, am a fan. My elder stoner cousin handed me his copy of Rush's magnum opus, 2112, when I was seven years old to take back to Virginia after our yearly vacation in Chicago. At the time, I was mostly listening to Beatles and KISS records, so Rush's prog rock skill and mastery were a whole new universe to my inexperienced ears. I was piqued. But it was the percussion on that album that really stuck out to me. It was the first time I'd heard them in the forefront of a song, as poetic and melodious as the vocals or guitar. I couldn't play what Neil Peart was doing, but I could FEEL it. Taylor Hawkins and I were requested to induct Rush into the Rock and Roll Hall of Fame and to perform the opening tune on 2112, an instrumental named "Overture" (no easy task). I'd met bassist Geddy Lee and guitarist Alex Lifeson throughout the years, both of whom were totally down-to-earth and outrageously funny, but never Neil Peart. Neil was more elusive, which was fair given that he was one of the greatest drummers of all time (not just in rock).

YET AGAIN, I AM INSPIRED.
Years later, I was given the opportunity to play drums on a tune with Elton on the Queens of the Stone Age album... The song, "Fairweather Friends," was a furious, unorthodox multipart composition that we had meticulously rehearsed before his visit, because Queens usually recorded full band live to tape, which meant you had to have your shit together and get it right. "Okay, boys, what?" replied Elton, fresh from a session with Engelbert Humperdinck (no joke). "Do you have a ballad for me?" We all laughed and exclaimed, "No... Come listen." It would be impossible for anyone to walk in and learn such a hard song right away, but

Elton sat at the piano and WORKED on it until he got it right, take after take, ever the perfectionist, proving why he is the queen bitch of rock and roll.

YET AGAIN, I AM INSPIRED.
It's the moments with no safety net that keep your spirits up, and if you're an explorer like me, you can always find those moments. And most of the time in the most unexpected places. Our tour manager, Gus, informed us one night in Osaka that Huey Lewis would be attending the show. "HUEY, LEWIS!!!" Pat exclaimed loudly. I had never seen him so animated in all my years of knowing him. Pat utterly demolished my idea of him as the punkest motherfucker on the earth by informing me that the album Sports by Huey Lewis and the News was one of his favorite recordings of all time (along with Butterfly by Mariah Carey). Taylor then informed me that Huey actually played harmonica on Thin Lizzy's Live and Dangerous record, which I had no idea about but now makes sense.

Huey emerged, and the backstage was soon buzzing with our regular beer and whiskey pre-show ritual. Take it from me, Huey is a fantastic hang. We drank, smoked, and laughed, and I ultimately inquired about his relationship with Phil Lynott and Thin Lizzy (great band). He told me about his harmonica solo on that song and how he, too, was a fan of Thin Lizzy. By the fifth song, I noticed Huey, beaming and waving his harp in the air. He leapt out next to me and started to shred a solo with a plastic harmonica purchased from a Japanese toy store on a Sunday night that would make the man from Blues Traveler throw down his bandoliers and flee to his mama. I was completely taken aback. This dude is a grade A, 100 percent badass motherfucker, and I will never again question the legitimacy of Sports. I'm sorry. For one night only, we were "Huey Lewis and the Foos," and I enjoyed it.
ANOTHER TURN IN A PREVIOUSLY WINDING PATH.
You never know who might come on the side of the stage, so strike while the iron is hot. Years ago, the BBC requested us to record a cover song, which we like and do frequently, building a repertoire of tunes you never imagined you'd hear the Foo Fighters play (or attempt to do). We were on tour at the time, but we were supposed to record it as soon as we got back home, so we had to pick a song and

have it ready to go within a few days. Taylor and I sat in our tiny warm-up area backstage at Tokyo's Summer Sonic music event, playing around with a few ideas, when I discovered Rick Astley was also on the list.

Pat, Chris, Rami, our keyboardist, and Nate joined in, and before long, the two tunes were virtually indistinguishable, like a hellish mash-up. It was so hilarious and absurd that we did it again and again, until Gus walked in and informed us it was time for the show. We took the enormous stadium stage and launched into our regular barn burner set, but after a few songs, I noticed a familiar figure by the monitor board stage right. It was Rick fucking Astley, rocking out to the band in the distance, his unmistakable boyish face bobbing up and down. I approached Rami and offered my hand during one of his keyboard solos. "We just learned 'Never Gonna Give You Up' half an hour ago," I remarked over the crushing noise of the show going on behind me. "Would you like to join us?" He was stunned but responded without hesitation, "Fuck yes," and within seconds he was onstage singing with a slew of strangers in front of fifty thousand puzzled Japanese Foo Fighters fans, flying by the seat of his trousers.

Meeting a musician who has inspired you is not the same as meeting a musician who has no personal relevance in your life. That's an intriguing juxtaposition. Whereas I've melted into a puddle when I've met the most obscure, unknown, underground hardcore musicians, I've also been as cool as a cucumber when I've met luminaries whose music never became a part of my vocabulary. Not to suggest Neil Diamond isn't a god among men, but the "Sweet Caroline" single wasn't on my Venom and Dead Kennedys records as a kid, so when we met at the 2009 MusiCares tribute, where he was being recognized, I just thought he was a really nice guy. But there was one person I knew would melt into a puddle upon seeing him, and that was the mother of my late buddy Jimmy Swanson. And she was the reason we were there. That weekend, I was on double duty, playing drums for Paul McCartney at the Grammys, where we blasted through a wonderfully raw version of "I Saw Her Standing There," so Mary Jane flew out and joined us, going from sitting on the couch in her TV room to sitting in an arena with Kid Rock, U2, and Stevie Wonder.

The following night was Mary Jane's great chance to finally meet her idol, Neil Diamond. I had met him earlier in the day backstage, and he was a vision of seventies cool, with his red silk shirt with diamonds embroidered on the collar (which we all congratulated him on), immaculate hair, and a voice that would make anyone weak in the knees. I explained the emotional significance of the occasion, and he graciously agreed to come say hello to Mary Jane after the show. And the next day, Mary Jane went back to Virginia, carefully packing that red silk shirt with diamonds embroidered on the collar in her suitcase. Neil Diamond had, indeed, given her the shirt off his back. Why are these people so important to me? Because people inspire others, and they have all become a part of my DNA through the years. Each and every note I've heard them play has shaped me in some manner. My memories have been painted with their voices as the frame.

I recall my uncle Tom taking me sailing when I was a kid, and we spent the day listening to—you guessed it—"Sailing" by Christopher Cross. If this hadn't been such a formative experience, I might not have tackled a terrified Christopher Cross at the Austin, Texas, airport baggage claim one day just to see him in person. Or the time I approached Ace Frehley of KISS on a Hollywood street corner late at night for a simple handshake, or shyly proclaimed my love to Bonnie Raitt as we sat on the Rock and Roll Hall of Fame's dressing room floor. BECAUSE I STILL WALK THROUGH LIFE LIKE A LITTLE BOY IN A MUSEUM, SURROUNDED BY THE EXHIBITS I'VE SPENT A LIFETIME STUDYING, AND I AM THANKFUL WHEN I FINALLY COME FACE-TO-FACE WITH SOMETHING OR SOMEONE WHO HAS INSPIRED ME ALONG THE WAY. I AM THANKFUL.

But meeting a hero in passing is one thing. It's quite another when they become your friend. I was walking toward the restroom of the seedy bar we were currently destroying with my crew years ago in Los Angeles when I noticed the one and only Lemmy sitting in the corner, drinking alone in front of a video poker machine (I won't say

his last name or band affiliation because if you don't already know
then I have to break up with you). I couldn't help myself. This man
was the live, breathing embodiment of rock & roll, and I had admired
him since the first time I heard his gravelly voice blasting through
my speakers. "Excuse me, Lemmy?" I said as I approached him.
just wanted to thank you for all of your years of inspiration.
"Cheers," he hissed from beneath his black cowboy hat, in a thick
cloud of Marlboro smoke. I was going to turn and walk away when
he replied, "Sorry 'bout your friend Kurt." Lemmy was no longer
globally revered rock and roll god after that; he was a fellow human
being. We became friends over hundreds of smokes and bottles of
Jack Daniel's throughout the years, swapping gruesome tales of life
on the road and a mutual love of Little Richard. I admired his
honesty, candor, and strength, as well as his fragility.
I was shocked to learn of his death. It had just been a few days since
his seventieth birthday and a few weeks since his last performance.
had assumed he would outlive all of us. He followed a difficult path
that most would not survive, and though it took its toll on him later
in life, he had the vigor and spirit of a warrior. Lemmy would not
give up until he had no choice but to surrender and rest.
immediately rushed to a tattoo parlor and branded my left wrist with
an ace of spades and the words "SHAKE YOUR BLOOD," a phrase
from a song we'd written together years before. He was a passionate
rock and roll fan who lived life to the fullest, two qualities we
definitely shared.

I was asked to speak at his memorial service a week or two later, and
while holding back tears, I told a few memories about our time
together to the small church full of his closest friends. This was a
bittersweet celebration of his life, because he had provided us all so
much joy but was now leaving us to face life without his priceless
friendship. I stood, taking out the small black-and-white photo that
Little Richard had autographed for me years before from my jacket
pocket, and read the words of an old gospel hymn that Little Richard
had once performed, "Precious Lord, Take My Hand."
Take My Hand."
Precious Lord, take my hand
Lead me on, let me stand
I am tired, I am weak, I am worn

Through the storm, through the night
Lead me on to the light
Take my hand, precious Lord
Lead me home
I turned and placed the picture on Lemmy's altar to thank him.
Forever grateful for the inspiration.

PART 5
LIVING

CHAPTER 1
Joan Jett's Bedtime Stories

"Hey, Harper... hey, Violet... what's the deal?"
My two kids sat in startled silence as Joan Jett, the one and only Queen of Rock and Roll, stood at the foot of the couch. She cast a long shadow over their cherubic faces with her spiky black hair, old Converse Chucks, and tight jean jacket, her distinctive gravelly voice shouting above the sound of the afternoon cartoons in the background. On a European visit a few months ago, I decided to take my girls to the massive London department store Harrods on a wet day off for some rug-rat shopping therapy. It was too cold for the park and too rainy for a walk, so I decided to take them on a tour of its famed toy department, which dwarfed most American toy stores, so they could get out of the hotel and have some fun. I know that it is not as culturally gratifying as visiting one of the city's many beautiful museums, but sometimes you simply have to say "Fuck it" and give the people what they want. Especially for people under four feet tall. As much fun as traveling the world with your family can be, keeping the kids entertained from one hotel room to the next becomes a mission over time, and you find yourself constantly researching activities days in advance to avoid falling into a vicious cycle of room service chicken fingers and subtitled cartoons.

I've joyfully watched my children progress from car seats strapped onto airplanes and bassinets next to hotel beds to waving down flight attendants for more ginger ale and ordering room service ice cream sundaes at midnight. They are now seasoned travelers, which I appreciate because it means we can stay together. To be honest, I soon found myself hooked in the LEGO department, swooning over the massive range on offer and debating whether I should participate in the challenge or remain a conscientious objector. I admit that I've always had a thing for LEGOs. They have always been my favorite toy since I was a child. I could spend hours upon hours building castles, vehicles, and other geometric buildings with their intricate small components and the satisfying snap of two tiny blocks fitting precisely together, just for the satisfaction of knowing that I had done it myself.

As the time approached, I issued a five-minute warning to the females in my best game-show presenter voice. Both, predictably, had yet to discover a toy and were still racing back and forth across the showroom floor, looking for the ideal reward. How could they possibly make a decision? I gave them "the look" (head bowed, one eyebrow arched) and repeated myself: "Five. Minutes." They had restricted their search to the Barbie portion, which was roughly the size of a big commercial airplane hangar at this stage. They circled, looking for their victim. This was not going to be simple. Hundreds of different Barbies lined the shelves, in all styles and themes, some with accessories, some with extra wardrobe... It was enough to blow any kid's mind. "TIME'S UP!" If only I'd had a whistle, I'd have yelled like a Little League official. "But, DAAAAAAD!!!!" they both exclaimed, frustrated. "We can't decide what to get!" "Come on!" I exclaimed, laughing. Choose one, any one, and let's go back to the hotel!" I looked down at the table next to me, which was piled high with Barbies, and grabbed the first one I could find. "Look! I got a Barbie!" I said, waving it in the air. "It's not fair!" "You can't get a Barbie!" they yelled back, and as I looked at the box, I realized I'd unintentionally purchased an actual Joan Jett Barbie, replete with red Converse Chucks, leather jeans, a sleeveless black T-shirt, and a white Gibson Les Paul Junior guitar draped over her shoulder. I thought to me, Holy sh*t. I'm absolutely going to buy this! We were all standing at the checkout line, comparing our Barbies (Rocker Joan and two super-tricked-out glam women with tons of accessories), eager to get back to the hotel and play.

Later that night, as I sat at my desk in our suite's living room, Violet and Harper entered and respectfully requested if they may play with my Barbie. "Of course!" says the author. I smiled as I carefully opened the colorful box, surgically detaching the doll from its outrageously intricate packing (since when do toys require a degree in engineering to get them out of their fucking packages? I realized the girls had no idea Joan Jett was a real person as they patiently watched me struggle with each small zip tie. They mistook her for another plastic figurine, one of hundreds on the shelves of their new favorite toy store. I came to a halt, set down the doll, and explained that Joan was not only a real person, but a very important one.

A FEMINIST ICON WHO DEMONSTRATED TO THE WORLD THAT WOMEN CAN ROCK HARDER THAN MEN. She was an architect, an innovator, and a punk rock pioneer so powerful that she encouraged generations of young women to pick up guitars and do the same. They were perplexed, so I opened my laptop, turned up the volume to ten, and played the "I Love Rock 'n Roll" video for them. We ultimately made our way to New York City for a gig at Madison Square Garden, one of my favorite venues in the world, as the tour progressed. The drive into the building reminded me of a scene from Led Zeppelin's live concert film The Song Remains the Same, which I literally studied as a teenager, unsuccessfully trying to decipher John Bonham's superhuman drumming. Pat Smear, our founding guitarist and reigning cool minister, knew Joan from his days with the iconic band the Germs. Pat, who was born and raised in Los Angeles, was a punk rock child in the mid-1970s and a major fan of Joan's first band, the Runaways, an all-girl group raised on Bowie and T-Rex. He'd seen all of their gigs and eventually became friends with Joan, as part of a gang of Hollywood punks who would unintentionally impact the path of music forever.

Pat, who was roughly the same age as Joan at the time, was so inspired by the Runaways that he and his best buddy, Darby Crash, decided to form their own band. When it came time to record their first full-length studio album, GI, in 1979, they enlisted the help of Joan Jett. So there was a rich history there, not only in rock & roll history, but also personally. We practiced the song on practice instruments in our dressing rooms and added it to the conclusion of the set list, knowing it would undoubtedly be the highlight of the evening. Joan was a joy to be around, her murderous sneer replaced by a smile bright enough to light up Madison Square Garden on its own, and seeing her and Pat reunited after all these years thrilled my heart. Who knows where we would be without these two? I felt like an extra in a documentary that I would gladly pay to see.

Joan's presence, by the way, cannot be underestimated. I was standing in a huge corridor full of people before the show, catching up with old friends over cocktails, when Joan discreetly emerged from our dressing room. As she slowly strolled down the corridor alone, like a post-apocalyptic James Dean, I watched every last person, men and women alike, hug the walls, truly stunned in her wake. She sliced a way through the throng one stride at a time, inducing a collective swoon that perhaps only Elvis could match. This was real rock and roll. Joan was, in fact, a superhero. I couldn't wait to tell my girls that not only was their favorite superhero coming to Los Angeles to write with me, but he was also staying with us for the weekend! Their imaginations would be completely blown! It's a lot for a youngster to fully appreciate breaking the fourth wall in life, when the dream of toys and YouTube videos becomes reality. Violet was only five years old, and Harper was just two. Nonetheless, I did everything I could to prepare them for Joan's arrival, hoping that it wouldn't send them into a tailspin. I mean, I'm sure you'd be surprised if Spongebob SquarePants came up at your front door.

We arrived home that night after a wonderfully fruitful day, and I began my regular ritual of getting my girls ready for bed while Joan went to the guesthouse to change into her jammies (yes, she wore pajamas, just when I thought she couldn't be much cuter). I bathed Harper, changed her into PJs, read her a couple tales, and placed her in her cot without a cry. One completed, one to go. Violet was the next to arrive. Before putting her to bed, I took her down to the living room to say good night to Joan. As I watched the two walk upstairs hand in hand, I prayed that Violet would never forget this moment, that she would look back on this night and realize that some superheroes are real. That maybe one day she'll be her own kind of innovator, an architect, a trailblazer, motivating generations of young ladies to pick up a guitar or do whatever she wants to do to make her mark.
EVERY GIRL NEEDS A JOAN JETT IN A WORLD FULL OF BARBIES.

CHAPTER 2
The Daddy-Daughter Dance

The Dance of the Daddy and Daughter
"Oh, by the way... this year's daddy-daughter dance is on March 6th. Make a note of it on your calendar."
As my wife's voice resonated through the exaggerated delay of long-distance call from Los Angeles to my hotel room in Cap Town, South Africa, my heart froze. I thought to myself, "March sixth?" Oh, please make that a day off at home... The daddy-daughter dance was a school custom that was nearly required for any parent trying to raise a girl in Los Angeles' Silicon Valley (no, I'm not referring to software). A chance to reinforce the family link, spend quality time together, and remind them that no matter what, a girl can always count on her loving old father. From kindergarten to sixth grade, it was an annual parade of middle-aged men in starched business suits doing their best to politely socialize with each other while their little girls, dressed in miniature ball gowns with corsages carefully pinned, ate candy hand over fist from long tables that would make Willy Wonka blush.

Deep down, I knew that these formative activities would undoubtedly serve as the foundation for many high school dances to come, therefore it was critical that they go successfully for my kid, or she would face an adolescence of proms akin to the bucket-of-blood scene from Carrie. But this year was different. Harper, who is three years Violet's junior, would constantly stand wailing at the door when Violet and I left for the dance, pleading to be invited even though she wasn't yet a student at the school. It crushed my heart to see her wave goodbye, pacifying her tears, unable to comprehend her ineligibility. "We'll all go together someday!" I'd always try to soothe her. Nonetheless, the sight of her standing at the doorway, tears running down her cheeks, holding her favorite blanket always hit me right in the gut. And now that she was old enough and I had the opportunity to fulfill my promise to take them both to the dance, something Harper had been looking forward to for nearly half her life, I had a fucking gig the same night—9,330 miles away.

Recognizing the gravity of the situation, we put on our thinking caps and began rearranging dates. They could surely get me to the Sportsmen's Lodge on time in my Levi's and filthy Clarks shoes if they could put a man on the moon, right? The tour, which was set to begin in Christchurch, New Zealand, was just eight gigs long, all in stadiums in the scorching summer heat. It was going to be our biggest trip to Australia yet, and tickets were going fast. We've always had a fiery love affair with our pals in New Zealand and Australia, making it a point to pay them a visit at least once every album cycle. And it's always well worth it. We had spent a decade exploring this heavenly territory, making lifelong friends and rocking the fuck out of every venue we set foot in, from the black pebble beaches of Piha, New Zealand, just outside of the cosmopolitan wonderland of Auckland, to the wineries surrounding the hills of Adelaide, Australia. The Perth show, which was already sold out, could be moved to the eighth, giving me just enough time to run offstage in Adelaide, board a chartered plane to Sydney, immediately jump on a Qantas flight back to L.A., land at LAX, sleep a few hours, take my girls to the dance, then leave straight from the Sportsmen's Lodge for the airport and fly back to Perth just in time to run onstage and kick their fucking asses.
CRAZY? PERHAPS. DOABLE? BARELY. MANDATORY? INDISPUTABLY.

By the time we arrived in Adelaide, our transcontinental operation had been meticulously planned down to the minute. My tour manager, Gus, and I were prepared to leap from the stage like soldiers from a Black Hawk helicopter and rush to a private plane waiting for us on a nearby tarmac, where we would be flown to Sydney to connect for the hard fifteen-hour flight home. To say the least, it was intimidating, but it was a hilarious task that we both looked forward to, giggling at the silliness of it all. That night's show was a ripper, a twenty-four-song blitz that had the stadium going bananas while I kept a tight eye on the clock on the side of the stage, making sure I gave the audience every last second of my time before I had to go. As the final chords of "Everlong" hung in the air, Gus and I hopped in a car and rushed off to a small local airport, eager to round the globe together.

As we boarded our first plane, the familiar aroma of a sizzling bucket of KFC wafted across the cabin. This was not an accident. The Foo Fighters have a strange indulgence that we occasionally request for rare occasions (and there are many special occasions): KFC and champagne. This delectable mix was discovered by accident on a previous tour of Australia. The two-hour trip to Sydney flew by quickly, giving us a few hours' layover before the long flight, just enough time to call home and inform the girls I was coming. I could sense their enthusiasm over the phone, and it was only a matter of hours before I saw them again. The excitement and adrenaline made the next flight seem endless, but my heart was full with fatherly pride as I pictured coming into the Sportsmen's Lodge with my two amazing kids, one on each arm. When I arrived in Los Angeles, I looked like I'd been hit by a garbage truck, but I was met by two wailing small girls as I went through the main door, a sensation that outlasted even the most intense jet lag. Knowing I only had a few hours with them, I avoided physical weariness and went into "dad mode."

I never went to school dances. They were terribly embarrassing experiences that just served to confirm my terrible inadequacies as a nerdy kid and never failed to tell me that I JUST CAN'T DANCE. The horrific routine of standing in a circle with pals trying to summon the funk while Rick James's "Super Freak" blasted over the PA has left me permanently scarred, deathly scared of any dance floor outside of the privacy of my own kitchen. Not to mention the homecoming dance on a boat, where I was tossed halfway down the Potomac River without a life jacket. So I became a wallflower. Perhaps paradoxical given that I have dedicated my life to rhythm. But I've seen a lot of drummers dance, and it's not pretty. This is a night the girls will remember for the rest of their lives, and you only have two hours to experience it with them before dashing back to the airport for another 10,000-mile flight. All it took was one glimpse at their amazing expressions to restore my strength. I WAS FILLED WITH PRIDE AGAIN, KNOWING THAT THEY COULD DEPEND ON ME NO MATTER WHAT. I'VE GOT IT.

As we walked into the main room, we were greeted with balloons, tables perfectly set with gorgeous dishes, a magnificent buffet of simple spaghetti and chicken nuggets, and a dance floor filled with screaming children. As we examined the landscape, our eyes lit up like Dorothy's as she entered the magical world of Oz, and we exchanged a group hug. I've always felt like an outsider, something I've grown to accept through time. When I was seven years old and was diagnosed with a crooked spine, I had to start wearing a little lift on my left shoe to gradually cure the problem. I recall feeling ashamed and embarrassed at first because I wasn't permitted to wear the cool sneakers that all the other kids wore, but that shame and humiliation eventually morphed into a sense of empowerment. I appreciated being different from them, even if it was just because of the shoes I wore. I didn't want to be the same as the other youngsters. I liked the feeling of being odd, no matter how crooked I was. They still do. So here I was, trying to fit in, always the kid with the strange sneakers.

I kept an eye on the clock, knowing that my fiendish itinerary left little room for error. Counting down the minutes until I had to say goodbye again (something I always dread), I opted to stop at the buffet for a Caesar salad, knowing that the food on the flight would be more to my liking. It was finally time. I scoured the room for my kids and fought back tears as I watched them having the time of their lives, bouncing and yelling with their friends and trying their hardest to nail the cha-cha slide. I drew them to the side and explained, in my best Courtship of Eddie's Father tone, that it was time for me to leave, expecting an outpouring of tears and crushing hugs. MY PRIDE WAS NOW THAT OF A FATHER WATCHING HIS DAUGHTERS DISCOVER INDEPENDENCE, NO LONGER CLINGING TO THEIR DOTING PARENT, BUT RATHER FINDING THEIR OWN WORLD BEYOND THE ONE WE HAD CREATED TOGETHER. My separation anxiety was entirely mine. I grabbed my jacket and dashed to the airport, leaving them with their mother to finish this crucial night. I replayed the past twenty-four hours in my thoughts as I sat in the airport lounge, blazing through a bottle of Shiraz, picking out moments that will certainly be with me forever.

Gus and I boarded the plane, and I stuffed my tired bones into the comfortable seat, passing off in a lovely red-wine haze before we ever took off. The mission has been completed. I convinced myself that it will pass. I've got it. After about twenty minutes, I felt a piercing pain in my stomach, like if someone had taken a knife and carved their initials into my intestines, as lovers do on park benches and ancient oak trees. This was out of the ordinary. This was not a case of motion sickness. A touring musician's biggest dread is food illness. You drink hot tea when you have a cold. You take medicine if you have the flu. If you get food poisoning, you are completely screwed. There is no way to prevent your body from doing what it is genetically programmed to do: puke and spit the poison out of you. But I have a greater issue. I am physically unable to vomit. Since the age of twelve, I've only thrown up three times: once at fourteen while listening to David Bowie's "Space Oddity" outside of a keg party (nothing worse than heaving up still-cold Meister Brau), once in 1997 after a bad piece of street pizza in Hollywood (seemed like a good idea at the time), and once in 2011 after seeing Soundgarden at the Los Angeles Forum (it wasn't the music). So any bout of sickness is usually accompanied by a lengthy process of convincing myself that I have this. It's basically my hell.

The flight that followed was a nightmare. Multiple trips to the restroom, all of which were unsuccessful, and then back to my seat for another round of spasmodic chills and fever. There was no sleep. There is no rest. Just a never-ending worst-case scenario that couldn't have happened at a worse time, given that I had to head straight to the gig for soundcheck after landing in Perth. This was a test, I reasoned. A test of determination, perseverance, and the age-old adage "You do what you have to do to get to the gig." A basic yes-or-no form with a list of symptoms that could indicate Ebola infection. I cringed as I read the list. Nausea. Diarrhea. Fever. The chills... I was displaying every single one of them. My imagination flashed back to being thrown in an airport room with true Ebola patients, where I would get the disease and eventually die alone in the land Down Under. I sat up in my chair, put on my best game face, and wished my illness away. This was not the end; it had just begun. As we walked to baggage claim, his phone rang, and he began rushing, as he always did, to find a solution to fix this most catastrophic situation. Our grand scheme had been derailed, all bets were off, and it had now devolved into a rock and roll version of The

Amazing Race. What had seemed like a ludicrous adventure at first was now a fundamental survival struggle. All in the father's name.

Gus had arranged for a doctor to meet me at the hotel in Perth by the time we took our next flight. Fortunately, the worst of it looked to be past, and it was now just a matter of attempting to keep down some tea and toast, hoping that it would supply even a smidgeon of the energy that I would need to pull off another two-and-a-half-hour screaming rock extravaganza. That seemed like an insurmountable assignment, but there was no going back now. The stage was prepared, the gear was ready, and thousands of die-hard Foos fans were getting ready for the night of their lives. My fellow bandmates greeted me backstage with surprise. They had been told that I might be sick, so there were discussions about changing the set list and having emergency preparations in case I pulled a GG Allin and covered the stage in dirt. My regular pre-show ritual of jumping in place while joking with the guys over cocktails was reduced to sitting on the couch with a half-eaten banana in my hand, attempting to find the strength to sing out twenty-five songs in the July heat. What had the potential to be a career-defining train crash of historic proportions turned out to be a fantastic night of thunderous sing-alongs and jubilant end-of-tour celebration. The 36 hours leading up to this performance energized not only my body but also my soul, reminding me of all the things I am grateful for in my life. My household. My associates. This is my music. Life had healed me, and I returned to the hotel after the show, not broken but stronger, with one more fantastic Australian tour under my belt.

As I circled the earth one last time, I reflected on this audacious act of love for my children, thinking about my own connection with my father and wondered if he would have done the same for me. Would he have moved heaven and earth to be there for me on such a special day? Doubtful, I reasoned. Maybe I love so strongly as a father because my father couldn't. I am a firm believer that your understanding or "version" of love is acquired by example from the start, and it serves as your divining rod throughout life, for better or ill. A solid basis for all meaningful partnerships. My mother is unquestionably responsible for me. I LOVE MY CHILDREN AS I WAS LOVED AS A CHILD, AND I HOPE THAT WHEN THEIR

TIME COMES, THEY WILL DO THE SAME. CERTAIN CYCLES ARE DESIGNED TO BE BROKEN. SOME ARE SUPPOSED TO BE REINFORCED.

CHAPTER 3
The Wisdom of Violet

"Are you sitting down?" In this moment, John Silva's voice, terminally hoarse from decades of yelling orders from his cluttered Hollywood office, couldn't have been clearer. After all, no one wants to hear these four words at the start of a phone call, especially from the man in control of their career. "Yes... why, what is it???" As shock waves of terror and worry began to pulse through every vein in my body, I instantly yelled back, expecting some devastating news. "It was the Academy Awards. This year, they want you to play 'Blackbird' by yourself on the show." I came to a halt and my thoughts immediately went to the moment when all eyes and cameras would turn to me, alone with only an acoustic guitar, live on television in front of 34 million people. Even though I was wearing sweatpants in my home room and the show was weeks away, debilitating stage fear struck me immediately. I can't think of a more scary prospect. I could only manage a hushed "Holy shit!" in response.

Of course, I was familiar with the song. Since I was a child, I'd memorized the arrangement, and I'd eventually mastered Paul McCartney's sophisticated fingerpicking guitar style while singing along to his timeless melody. It's one thing to perform such a tough song from the luxury of your own couch at home. It's another thing entirely to do it while the WHOLE FUCKING PLANET is watching (not to mention Jennifer Lawrence and Sylvester Stallone).

Deep down, I was terrified. After all, "Blackbird" is no walk in the park, and performing at the Oscars is completely different than performing in front of a stadium full of Foo fans. Fortunately, I had already sung the song to a different audience. Violet's third-grade Student Entertainment Day the previous year. Student Entertainment Day used to be a cavalcade of children performing piano recitals or lip-syncing along to Katy Perry songs with intricately choreographed dance routines for a gymnasium full of helicopter parents dressed in Lululemon activewear. Violet had raced home after hearing the news that year and excitedly asked if she might perform "Sgt. Pepper's

Lonely Hearts Club Band" with a bunch of her closest pals. By her standards, this was not an unusual request, since I had made it a point to brainwash her with the Beatles' whole catalog from a young age, aiming to create some type of solid musical foundation before she went on to Cardi B and Iggy Azalea.

Violet was saddened to learn that her pals would not be able to attend the event. The protective father in me kicked in as we sat on the couch together, watching the tears slide down her cherubic little face. "How about you and I do 'Blackbird' together?" I'll play the guitar while you sing!" She looked up and wiped her cheeks, and her expression suddenly turned to one of excitement and relief. I dashed to get my guitar, sat down in front of her, and began playing the song. She arrived on time, in tune, and we performed it together brilliantly on the first try, with no rehearsal or lyric sheet to refer to. It was stunning. I'd want to say I was surprised, but I wasn't. I knew she was capable. Could I, though? We high-fived and devised a strategy: we'd rehearse every morning before school and every night before bed until the gig, ensuring that we'd be more than ready when we took the stage.

Saturday Night Live, Wembley Stadium, the White House—each of these huge performances was a highlight of my career, but none compared to how nervous I was for this event. It didn't matter that it was merely a gymnasium full of parents sipping iced nonfat lattes and fiddling with their cell phones. I was there to support Violet, and the success of her performance was critical. So, from that day forward, I spent every spare time preparing to be her impeccable musical accompaniment, striving to master that exquisite guitar arrangement until I had blisters on every finger. I THOUGHT THIS WAS THE MOST IMPORTANT GIG OF MY LIFE. We arrived for soundcheck on the morning of the event, well-dressed and prepared. I asked for a stool to sit on while I played. Violet requested a music stand for her lyrics, just in case she needed them. We checked the guitar and microphone levels before waiting for the room to fill up. Violet had been at this school since kindergarten and knew almost everyone, but her incredible singing voice had been a well-kept secret, and it was about to be unleashed on this most unsuspecting audience.

Our names were called after a few adorable performances, and we climbed the stage to a sprinkling of applause. We took our seats and settled in, and in the terrifying pin-drop silence, I asked Violet, "Ready, Boo?" She nodded, terrified, and I began the delicate guitar prelude, telling myself that this was, without a doubt, the most significant performance of my life, as well as hers. As always, she arrived perfectly on time and in tune, and I watched as the audience's collective jaws began to drop. The room was astonished as her innocent, crystalline voice filled the PA. I couldn't help but smile as I realized they were finally meeting the Violet I knew so well. We were greeted with deafening applause and a standing ovation as the final chord rang out. We took a bow, high-fived, and handed the stage over to the next act. "You absolutely nailed it, Boo!" I said this while hugging her.

My heart was brimming with pride. Violet is proud of her musical ability, but she is also proud of her bravery. Courage is a defining characteristic of any artist. The guts to disclose your true voice, or to stand in front of an audience and lay it all out there for the world to see. The emotional openness required to summon a great song can also work against you when sharing your song with the rest of the world. Any sensitive artist faces this crippling dilemma. I waited for Violet to get home from school to deliver her the news, still undecided about the Academy Awards. I'd eventually decided to decline after much deliberation, convinced myself that I didn't need to play the Oscars and that I'd probably muck the entire thing up anyway, but I thought I'd share the insanity of the offer with my daughter. The gauntlet has been thrown. I realized in an instant that I had to win the Oscars. As her father, I now had to demonstrate to her that, no matter how afraid I was, I had the same courage that she had summoned in the gymnasium that day. OF COURSE, I HAD TO PROVE IT TO HER, BUT DEEP DOWN, I ALSO HAD TO PROVE IT TO MYSELF.

I called John Silva, accepted the offer, and started preparing for the most important performance of my life. It was determined that I would perform the song with an orchestra as a photo montage was presented above me. But there was a catch: the song had been completely altered to correspond with the photo sequence, and the orchestra was to be piped in from a studio down the street, leaving me alone on stage with no conductor to refer to if I needed help keeping up with the constantly fluctuating speed. As a result, I had to play to a "click track" via an ear monitor, which would serve as a metronome reference. Isn't it simple? Fun fact: I don't own and have never used in-ear monitors (earbud-like devices that assist you hear yourself and have become industry standard over the years). I still love old-school floor monitors that look like old speakers and blow your hair back with every kick drum hit. As a result, this constituted a major difficulty. How was I going to pull this off without a conductor to look at or a click track to follow?

I eventually caved and unwillingly agreed to utilize an in-ear monitor for the first time in my life in front of 34 million people. What did I get myself into? I pondered. I determined that in the event of a train wreck, I would just find Jennifer Lawrence in the front seat and serenade her as best I could. In a pinch, Sylvester Stallone will suffice. The Academy Awards are the worst of all award ceremonies. You almost need Pentagon clearance merely to plug in your instrument, and the process of being "dressed" is straight out of Cinderella. That's not how I feel. I'm used to walking into a party after a few cocktails wearing a blazer that's appropriate for both funerals and court hearings. But this was unique. I was quickly scheduled for a fitting at a Beverly Hills boutique to get the ideal suit. To put it mildly, I was a fish out of water.

I had no idea where to begin as I stood in front of the clothing racks. Anyone who knows me knows that I am the least trendy person on the planet and still dress as I did in ninth school (Vans, jeans, band T-shirt), so I was assigned a stylist to help me buy and fit the right suit. Kelsey, a stylish young blond woman with enormous blue eyes, was quickly presented to me. "We've actually met before," she said. I stared at her face, and while it appeared familiar, I couldn't identify it. "I was the little girl in Nirvana's 'Heart-Shaped Box' video..." Silence. Then I noticed it in those wide, blue eyes. It had to be her.

Mind. Fucking. Blown. THE UNIVERSE WAS WORKING HARD.

That video, created by famed photographer Anton Corbijn and shot twenty-three years previously, was a surrealist mosaic of birth, death, anatomy, and chaos set in a fantasy world with an elderly guy hanging on a cross in a Jesus Christ posture. A tiny girl in a white hood and robe stood in the middle of it all, her large eyes full of melancholy, possibly a metaphor of the innocence Nirvana had lost with our catastrophic journey to popularity. And now we were back together in a fitting room, fastening the cuffs of the jeans I'd be wearing while singing a Beatles song to a room full of movie stars. Isn't it ironic?

I would continuously return to the vision of Violet onstage, demonstrating to myself that she had the bravery to disclose her genuine voice, stand in front of an audience, and lay it all out there for the world to see. Her bravery inspired me, so I found my own and dedicated this performance to her in my heart. Take it from me: watching the Oscars from your living room with some spinach dip and a frosty Coors Light is far more fun. I admire anyone who spends their lives in the arts, but it felt like the longest Catholic Mass imaginable, minus the crackers and thimbles of cabernet. And my performance was at the end of the program, leaving me to deal with my mounting nervousness. Hours had gone. Weeks, not days. I was finally called onstage to prepare after what felt like an eternity.

During a commercial break, I stepped out to my chair in the middle of the stage, looking down in the front row, where Jennifer Lawrence and Sylvester Stallone had been sitting all night, searching for their faces to save me if I choked up and my performance went downhill. They were gone, replaced by seat fillers who all looked at me with puzzled expressions, presumably anticipating Lady Gaga. "One minute!" yelled a director over the PA. I inserted my tiny ear monitor, adjusted the microphone, exhaled deeply, and closed my eyes. Violet caught my eye. I witnessed her first steps as a baby. I watched her waving farewell to me on her first day of school. For the first time, I witnessed her pedaling away on a bicycle, no longer requiring the support of her adoring father. And I witnessed her perform "Blackbird" in the school gymnasium. I FELT HER BRAVENESS AND FOUND MY OWN. Unfortunately, Jennifer and Sly were unable to attend.

Printed in Great Britain
by Amazon

32576691R10059